Aaron Douglas
*Murals in the Countee
Cullen Branch of the
New York Library*

◀ One

◀ Two

Turn to back end-paper
for Panels 3 and 4, and
description by the artist

AMERICAN
NEGRO ART

Charles White
One of a series of
ink drawings based
on the spirituals
1958
Courtesy Harry Belafonte
Photograph: *Walter Rosenblum,*
New York City

CEDRIC DOVER

American Negro

NEW YORK GRAPHIC SOCIETY

Art

Richmond Barthé   *The Negro Looks Ahead*

ALAIN LOCKE (1886–1954)
Professor of Philosophy in Howard University, Washington, D.C., cultivator of all the Negro arts, and the 'onlie begetter', almost, of the New Negro
Portrait by Betsy Graves Reyneau
Courtesy of the Harmon Foundation, New York

Betsy Graves Reyneau represents an increasing number of white artists who have concerned themselves sympathetically and interestingly with the Negro people. Unfortunately this book permits no more than a hint of the grateful good language we owe them.

Cloth Edition: ISBN 0-8212-0101-8
Paperback Edition: ISBN 0-8212-1112-9
L C No. 60-51364

© Copyright 1960 by Cedric Dover
First published in hardcover in 1960 by Studio Books, now Studio Vista Ltd., London, and by New York Graphic Society Ltd., Greenwich, Connecticut.
Reprinted 1965, 1967, 1969, 1970
First published in paperback in 1970

Made in England

ACKNOWLEDGEMENTS

MY GRATEFUL ACKNOWLEDGEMENTS TO: W. E. Burghardt Du Bois and Shirley Graham (Mrs Du Bois), friends and mentors, for the frequent pleasure of sitting at their table—in more ways than one. Every book on Negro culture and affairs begins with Dr Du Bois;

The memory of Charles Houston, Charles Johnson, James Weldon Johnson, Alain Locke, Arthur Schomburg and Carter Woodson, whose friendship extended to letting me share what I could contain of their wisdom.

Arna Bontemps, Sterling Brown, John Hope Franklin, E. Franklin Frazier, Marie Frazier, Langston Hughes, Georgia Douglas Johnson, Rayford Logan, Aubrey Pankey, Eslanda Robeson and Paul Robeson, for taking me, through the written and spoken word over many years, farther into the American Negro scene. An additional acknowledgement is due to Langston Hughes, and to Alfred A. Knopf Inc., New York City, for borrowings from *The Weary Blues*.

The artists who introduced me to Negro art before the War: Alonzo Aden, Henry Bannarn, Richmond Barthé, Aaron Douglas, James Herring, James Porter, James Lesesne Wells and Hale Woodruff.

Harold Jackman, New York City, old friend and connoisseur of the arts, for forwarding a stream of letters and providing invaluable information. His co-operation has been basic.

Carl Van Vechten, New York City, who overcame a heat wave to print a large number of photographs of artists from his unique pictorial documentation of Negro personalities. He also took new photographs, several in colour, of artists and their works.

Alonzo Aden, Director of the Barnett Aden Gallery, Washington, D.C., whose critical sponsoring of Negro art and artists has created successions of fresh opportunities, directions and insights. The text and plates which follow have benefited greatly from his interest.

Mary Beattie Brady, Director of the Harmon Foundation, New York City, whose help with photographs, articles and advice goes back to 1938. The study of modern Negro art begins at the Harmon Foundation.

Helen Coulborn, Chairman of the Art Exhibition, Atlanta University, Atlanta, Georgia, who not only mailed packets of photographs, catalogues and bulletins, but also answered innumerable inquiries. Atlanta is an indispensable centre of Negro art today.

Tom Jones, Director of the Department of Arts and Sciences, International Business Machines Corporation, New York City, who supplied superb photographs of most of the small but excellent collection of American Negro art owned by the I.B.M.

James Porter, Professor of Art in Howard University, Washington, D.C., who provided what he could from the University's Gallery of Art and encouraged some of his students to send examples of their work.

Dorothy Homer, Supervising Librarian in the Countee Cullen Branch of the New York Public Library, who sent photographs of its many treasures.

R. Lynn Baker, New York City, for permission to reproduce Edmonson's *Preacher*, colour photographs of it *in situ*, and much friendly interest; Harold Benjamin, Harrow, Middlesex, for the loan of a print of Hale Woodruff's *Returning Home*; Arnold Gingrich, New York City, for permission to reproduce Pippin's *The Den* and for a large folder of *Esquire* cartoons by Elmer Simms Campbell; Marjorie Griesser of The Viking Press, New York City, for many efforts to find elusive artists and difficult pictures; Peter Nelken, Chief Editor of *Eulenspiegel*, Berlin, for a nation-wide search to provide an essential out-of-print book; Roy Neuberger, New York City, for photographs and permission to reproduce Pippin's *Cabin in the Cotton*; Harper Phillips, Grambling, Louisiana, for a special effort to secure photographs from Hampton Institute, Virginia, after he had left its Art Department; Roswell P. Russell, Baltimore, for permission to reproduce Joshua Johnston's *Mrs Moale* and information about the painter; and Hubert Giles and Ernest Wagner, Dillard University, New Orleans, for photographs of Julien Hudson's *Colonel Fortier* in the Louisiana State Museum, as well as a series of photographs, taken with the co-operation of Henri Gandolfo of the Albert Weiblen Marble and Granite Company, New Orleans, of works by Daniel Warburg.

The American Society of African Culture, New York City (George Carter); The Art Institute of Chicago (Anselmo Carini); The Brooklyn Museum, New York (John Gordon); The Carlen Galleries, Philadelphia (Robert Carlen); The Carnegie Institute, Department of Fine Arts, Pittsburgh (Gordon Bailey Washburn); The Cincinnati Art Museum (Philip Adams); Contemporary Arts Incorporated, New York City (Emily Francis); Creative Artists Guild, New York City (Roland Turner and Bernadine Watson); Detroit Institute of Arts (Addison Page); Grand Central Art Galleries, New York City (Mary Blank); The Index of American Design, National Gallery of Art, Washington, D.C. (Judith Cousins and Ellen Feinberg); Clarence Laughlin, New Orleans; Pennsylvania Academy of the Fine Arts, Philadelphia (Loren Eiseley); Philadelphia Museum of Art (David Sellin and Gertrude Toomey); The Phillips Gallery, Washington, D.C. (Elmira Bier); The Museum of Modern Art, New York City (Willard Tangen); The National Archives, Washington, D.C. (Josephine Cobb); Janet Nessler Gallery, New York City (Janet Nessler); San Francisco Museum of Art (George Culler, Katherine Baker and John Humphrey); and the Whitney Museum of American Art, New York City (Rosalind Irvine), for small but important collections of photographs and other friendly help.

The British Museum, London (Bernard Ashmole and D. E. L. Haynes); Arna Bontemps, Librarian, Fisk University, Nashville, Tennessee; William Alden Brown, Providence, R.I.; Brown University, Providence, R.I. (John McIntyre); Carolina Art Association, Gibbes Art Gallery, Charleston, S. Carolina (Helen McCormack); Natalie Robinson Cole, Los Angeles; Ida Cullen Cooper, New York City; David H. H. Felix, Philadelphia; Frick Art Reference Library, New York City (Hannah Howell and Mildred Steinbach); Dr and Mrs W. W. Goens, Wilmington, Delaware; Hampton Institute, Hampton, Virginia (Joseph Brady); Illinois State Museum, Springfield (Thorne Deuel); Martha Jackson Gallery, New York (David Anderson); Sidney Janis Gallery, New York City (Sidney Janis); Eloise Jenkins, Morristown, N.J.; Joseph Kersey, Chicago; Thelma Kirkpatrick, Chicago; Emily Lowe Gallery, New York City (Ward Eggleston); Thelma Marshall, Gary, Indiana; Maryland Historical Society, Baltimore (F. Garner Ranney); Nationalmuseet, Copenhagen; The Newark Museum, New Jersey (William Gerdts and Jane Stroebel); Ohio College of Applied Science, Cincinnati (Clarence Koehn and Marjorie Richardson); Providence Art Club, Providence, R.I. (William Farnsworth); Rhode Island School of Design, Providence (John Maxon); State University of Iowa, Iowa City (Earl Harper and Fred Kent); Talladega College, Alabama (Arthur Gray); Tuskegee Institute, Alabama (Charles Trout); United States Information Service, London (Stefan Munsing, Sally Green and W. A. Dunn); University of Illinois, Urbana (C. V. Donovan); Virginia Historical Society, Richmond (John Melville Jennings); and Wilberforce University, Ohio (C. LeRoy Jordan), for particular photographs and useful information.

Albany Institute of History and Art, New York (Janet McFarlane); Barnes Foundation, Merion, Pennsylvania (Violette de Mazia); Dillard University, New Orleans (Ernest Wagner); Arnold Finkel Gallery, Philadelphia; James Ivy, New York City; Library of Congress, Washington, D.C. (Roy Basler, Virginia Daiker and Alice Parker); Charles Morris, London; Lawrence Reddick, Alabama State College, Montgomery; Sie und Er, Zurich (L. Keller); Smithsonian Institution, National Collection of Fine Arts, Washington, D.C. (Thomas Beggs); Unesco Courier, Paris (S. M. Koffler); University of Michigan, Museum of Art, Ann Arbor (Charles Sawyer); Walker Art Centre, Minneapolis (Dorothy Berge); and John Hay Whitney Foundation, New York City (Charles Jones), for printed materials and information.

Janet Warburg Altimus, New Orleans; The Marquis of Bute (through Nora Hair); Sander Davidson, Tulsa, Oklahoma; Walter Goldwater, University Place Bookshop, New York City; Edith Halpert, The Downtown Gallery, New York City; Harvard College Library, Cambridge, Massachusetts (Robert Haynes); John Davis Hatch, Norfolk Museum, Virginia; Lord Chamberlain's Office, London (Oliver Millar); Los Angeles County Museum, California

CHARLES S. JOHNSON (1893–1956)
President of Fisk University, Nashville, Tennessee, sociologist, sometime Editor of *Opportunity*, New York, and promoter of the Negro, old and new
Portrait by Betsy Graves Reyneau
Courtesy of the Harmon Foundation, New York

(William Osmun); L. Kevin Malley, Dublin; McMillen Incorporated, New York City (Martha Schneider); Minneapolis Institute of Arts, Minnesota (Inez Quinn); Museum of Fine Arts, Boston (Perry Rathbone); The National Art Association, Washington, D.C. (Ralph Beelke); The National Gallery, London (R. O. Tudor); The National Gallery of Art, Dublin (Thomas McGreery); Delia Pleasants, Towson, Maryland; Edouard Roditi, London and New York City; The Duke of Sutherland (through P. R. Nicoll); Victoria and Albert Museum, London (Trenchard Cox); and the Whitechapel Art Gallery, London (Ann Forsdyke), for helpful information.

The Associated Negro Press, Chicago (Claude Barnett); *The Courier Journal*, Louisville Kentucky (Cary Robertson); *The Crisis*, New York City (James Ivy); *The Pittsburgh Courier* (P. L. Prattis); and *The Times-Picayune*, New Orleans (John Foster), for encouragement and assistance.

May Evans for summarising the careers of over two hundred artists and bearing the frustration of not seeing her biographical work published.

Studio Books, and their Anthony Adams in particular, for almost cheerful patience with a self-fertilising project which has increased itself by four in course of production.

Audrey MacLean, Col MacLean and Sandy Philp, friends, physicians and properly quarrelsome critics, for taking into their warmth a writer in continuous need of vitamins—multiple and moral.

Maureen Dover, partner beyond a decade, for her share in the making of yet another book.
LONDON: APRIL 1960

Humbert Howard
Show Girl
OIL   1956

FOR AARON DOUGLAS

An epoch ago, at Tuskegee, you and William Dawson took me into the sick heartlands of Alabama to visit an ex-slave, Mr Baker, whom you were painting. I still see him hurrying across his proudly cultivated farm with outstretched hands. "Now I can see," he said, as you introduced your friend from a faraway corner of the coloured world, "us niggers is getting together at last."

This simple truth brought me to Negro America again after the War. I settled at Fisk University because Charles Johnson, to whom getting together was also important, knew my affection for it and offered the opportunity for "intensive minority living". You were there, insisting as always that the artist must reach out to life with poetry, courage and laborious craftsmanship; and I was fortunate, since we roomed in the same house, in sharing your pleasures, philosophy and prejudices up and down the stairs for over a year.

What I absorbed is in the sifting of this book. In so far as it is mine, and that is very little, it is for you—and for the memory of our lovely Alta. You will criticize it, of course, but you will recognize behind its intention the rugged figure of a grand old gentleman in Alabama who would, I think, have seen it as another token of getting-togetherness. He would have known that our camp ground is a mighty big place now.

Carl Van Vechten and Aaron Douglas with Richmond Barthé's bust of *George Washington Carver*, who devoted his life to the chemistry of native products in the South, presented by the sculptor to the Carl Van Vechten Gallery of Fine Arts, Fisk University, Nashville, Tennessee. *Courtesy of Fisk University.* Photograph: *A. Glenn Hanson, Nashville.*

THE ARTISTS

The imperfections and interferences of this book are mine. Otherwise, it is the work of the artists who made it. Among them, photographs, printed materials and other kindnesses were gratefully received from:

Frank Alston, Ophelia Andrews, William Artis, Henry Bannarn, Richmond Barthé, Romare Bearden, John Biggers, Charles Boyd, Elmer Brown, Margaret Taylor Burroughs, James Cameron, Elizabeth Catlett, Barbara Chase, Kitty Chavis, Claude Clark, Irene Clark, Ladybird Cleveland, William Compton, Eldzier Cortor, Virginia Cox, Ernest Crichlow, Allan Crite, Beauford DeLaney, Richard Dempsey, Aaron Douglas, David Driskell, Eugenia Dunn, Elton Fax, Tom Feelings, Allan Freelon, Rex Goreleigh, Melvin Green, Eugene Grigsby, Phillip Hampton, Gilbert Harris, June Hector, Charles Hodson, Alvin Hollingsworth, Earl Hooks, Humbert Howard, John Howard, Richard Hunt, Yvonne Hunt, Clifford Jackson, Frederic Jones, John Jones, Lois Mailou Jones, Allan Junier, Joseph Kersey, Hughie Lee-Smith, James Lewis, Romeyn Van Vleck Lippman, Geraldine McCullough, Samuel Middleton, Frank Moore, Lena Moore, Leedell Moorehead, Norma Morgan, Archibald Motley, Frank Neal, Hayward Oubré, Aubrey Pankey, James Parks, Marion Perkins, Harper Phillips, Delilah Pierce, Harold Pierce, James Porter, Tommie Price, Frank Rawlings, James Reed, Percy Ricks, Gregory Ridley, John Robinson, Walter Sanford, Ann Sawyer, Thomas Sills, Carroll Simms, E. Simms Campbell, Jewel Simon, Walter Simon, Merton Simpson, Marvin Smith, Charles Stallings, Douglas Staten, Lewis Stephens, William Taylor, Alma Thomas, Mildred Thompson, Dox Thrash, Roland Turner, William Walker, James Washington, James Watkins, Bernadine Watson, James Lesesne Wells, Charles White, Vivian Williams, Walter Williams, Stan Williamson, Ed Wilson, Ellis Wilson, John Wilson, Hale Woodruff, Roosevelt Woods.

Eldzier Cortor
Room No. V
OIL   1948
Courtesy Carnegie Institute, Pittsburgh

Contents

African Fantasy

Barry Place   *Woodcuts by James Lesesne Wells*

. . . one seed becomes
An everlasting song, a singing tree
Jean Toomer

Hale Woodruff
Totem

Courtesy the Artist

PERSPECTIVES

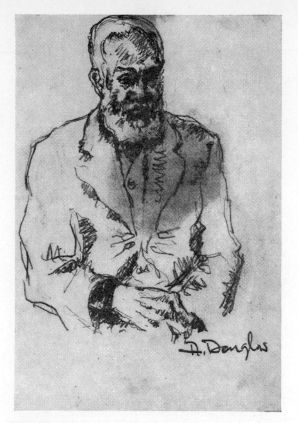

Aaron Douglas
Mr Baker
A Sketchbook Study

Mr Baker was a farming philosopher, who reached adolescence in slavery. It was a privilege to know him—as a person and as a symbol of the wise, courageous and creative ancestry of the Negro people of America

INTRODUCTION

History is no longer chronicled in verse, but peoples still speak through their poets. And, as artists are poets too, an anthology of the art of a people is a reflection, in poetic images, of their total experience.

The appreciation of the Negro minority in America should, accordingly, be enlarged by this picturebook of responses to needs, situations, surroundings and ideas. There is something in it of the tears, laughter, courage, awareness and zestful vigour with which the songs of 'black folk' are charged; but it moves more definitely into the future than the promise of a new day.

We get a glimpse, in fact, of the shape of Negro things to come. It should hold our attention, for the upsurge of the coloured peoples is one of the many tokens that we are now living with the necessity, rather than the dream, of one world.

In this situation, the importance of American Negroes goes far beyond the creative, economic and voting power of their sixteen millions. Their advances at home are assurances of the revival of humanism in America—and no prospect there is watched abroad with more friendly concern. Their progress, their influencing international positions, their many services to the Afro-Asian nations, also nourish the pride and hopes of all the coloured peoples, who will find here artistic evidence, with analogies for themselves, of the most striking ethnic adjustment since the Voyages of Discovery. Those others who are interested in 'colour problems', perhaps even those who chatter about 'race' as décor for their attentions to themselves, can look at it in much the same way.

The impact of the pictures as a collection will not, I think, be very differently felt; but what they communicate individually must depend on the eyes with which we see as well as their own artistic appeal. We can look, for example, at Archibald Motley's *Mending Socks* (plate 33), purely in pictorial terms (what that means I do not exactly know), or we can seek the poetic images that transform it. Then it can be emotionally interpreted in terms of universals—and the ultimate test of a successful work of art, whether academic or 'modern', is the emotional force of the images it projects. Therefore, preferences for representational art or otherwise have not guided the selection of pictures for this book. Some fell, without much choice, into a particular section of the broad design; a few were regretfully excluded because they would have suffered too much from reproduction in black and white.

11

THE BACKGROUND

The Negroes sold in the early slave markets of the New World were brought mostly from West Africa, where the arts were highly developed. Their languages were articulated with such delicately controlled variations of tone and timing that spoken words could be easily intensified into songs which gained rhythm from measured repetition—a universal folk-device which we know so well in the blues, spirituals and English shanties.

Their music translated the sound of words into drum languages, for the drum, when sounded with perfect physical co-ordination, is the ideal instrument for imitating the timed vibrations of speech and song. Their ritual mimetic dancing completed the unity of speech, song, music and bodily expression into integrated activities by all, not entertainments by a few, which gave fullness and the security of magic to personal and collective living.

Woodcarvers, bonecarvers and metalworkers supplied the necessary images, totem animals and other objects; weavers and designers of appliqué 'dressed the gods in fine clothes' by making the special costumes required for cult ceremonies; and all went beyond strictly traditional limits when serving the personal needs of their patrons. Thus, the products of the visual arts were also universals in tribal life; but their making was confined to gifted specialists, often organized in guilds, who gave pictorial quality to the control of nature and the unknown, supported tribal prestige, and perceptively adapted their skills to reducing new situations to manageable proportions.

The coming of white men created, of course, the newest and most disrupting situations; and, wherever they came, the tribal artists responded, as Julius Lips has shown, with humour and understanding. They comforted the distressed pride of their peoples by presenting the intruders as clowns or tricksters who wore strange hats, carried threatening muskets, drank goblets of strong liquor, and were so idle that they either rode short distances or were carried in hammocks or chairs.

But it was recognized that the virtues and intentions of some Europeans, however odd their appearance and behaviour, were admirable. They were accordingly portrayed with evident appreciation—none more so than the diminutive but ample queen who inspired African loyalties and hopes during the later years of the nineteenth century. Charmingly Africanized and clearly affectionate effigies of her can still be found.

These attempts at characterization, satirical or gracious, were developed by some African artists into the larger intention to contain the consequences of contact with Europeans in a single work of art. A token of their success is a spirally carved tusk, of truly remarkable workmanship and social understanding, in the Ethnographical Department of the National Museum at Copenhagen. It was acquired in 1880 at Lourenço Marques, once a notorious centre of the eastern slave trade, where the natives had long experience of the Portuguese and their Dutch enemies; and each spiral depicts a descending phase of that experience to the ultimate degradation of the coffle. The man who made it was a master.

The qualities that urged these fundamentally sad variations in African tribal art survived in the Americas with the slaves who survived—and the 'unpunishable Ethiopian' of Homer's day remained at least as unpunishable, in spite of considerable punitory talents, in the continent which Columbus and his black pilot, Alonzo, gave to European enterprise. Indeed, having come with the first colonists, it was soon recognized, as a Dutchman wrote from Surinam in 1663, that African slaves had become 'the strength and sinews of this western world'.

In the disorderly Jamestown Colony of Virginia, with which the continuous history of English America begins (1607), the servants who accompanied adventurous gentlemen included a coloured woman; and when John Rolfe was back in his tobacco fields there in 1619, having buried his young wife, the Princess Pocahontas, at Gravesend, he wrote in his diary the most picture-making sentence in early colonial history: 'About the last of August came in a Dutch man of warre that sold us twenty Negars.' Those Negars, and those brought in mounting numbers as the plantations grew and indigo, sugar, rice and cotton became additional cash crops, were the 'hands' that built the colonies, kept the planter-aristocracy in the governing ease to which they were not always accustomed, and maintained the expanding prosperity of the nation in which the enjoyment of plenty soon settled into the habit of 'conspicuous consumption'.

What is more noteworthy, since other civilizations have been founded on slavery, is that the mixture and setting of African culture patterns in the moulds of the plantation environment enriched America in many ways and gave it the only native folk music and dance since it was colonized. This well-known fact has been called a 'miracle', but it can be simply explained.

The men sold into slavery were mostly warriors taken in battle or associated with internal revolts, witch doctors who had become too ambitious, and

Hughie Lee-Smith
Festival's End

Courtesy Janet Nessler
Gallery, New York
Special photograph for this book
by Percy Rainford, New York City

others who had displeased their chiefs or brought them good prices—and these were the men usually most accomplished in singing and dancing. Moreover, their survival rate was high. Tough, or shrewd, or both, they were the most likely to live through the passage to the coast, the horrors of the slave ships, and their first days on the plantations.

There they started without the integrating benefits of their tribal cultures, for they were either distributed without regard for their origins or according to the old principle of divide and rule. They often spoke different languages, and many who did not come direct from Africa had no more language than a jumble of two or three; but they re-grouped themselves and naturally found in chanted verse, singing and dancing a means of survival. With a hint from the popular songs of the early seventeenth century, such as those of Thomas Ravenscroft, they could shape a rhyme like this:

Once dere wus er frog dat lived in er mill.
He had er raker don la bottom o' la kimebo,
Kimebo, nayro, dilldo, kiro,
Stimstam, formididdle, all aboard la rake,
Wid er raker don la bottom o' la kimebo.

More familiarity with spoken English brought out word-pictures reminiscent of tribal impressions in wood and metal:

Mosser is six foot one way, an' free foot tudder,
An' he weigh five hundred poun'.
Britches cut so big dat dey don' suit de tailor,
An' dey don' meet half way roun'.
Mosser's coat come back to a claw-hammer p'int
(Speak sof' or his bloodhoun'll bite us).
His long white stockin's mighty clean an' nice,
But a liddle mo' holier dan righteous.

An enormous body of secular rhymes and songs, rich in pointed comment, grew from these beginnings and still continues. Satire never gave way to the consolations of Christianity, but from the hope of a great camp meetin' in de Promised Lan', and from the images and parallels learned during the Sabbath, the slaves made the simple but moving poetry and the noble music of the spirituals—the only recreation of myth by an entire people in recent times.

They have been called sorrow songs by Dr W. E. B. Du Bois, and they are essentially sorrowful even when they are militant, for they spring from the kind of distress which can convert 'He gave up his soul to the stroke without a murmuring word' into a line recalling the whole *via crucis*: 'An' he nevah said a mumbalin' word.' But the transforming quality arises, too, from the African manner of singing, sometimes almost entirely from the familiar Negro

Ann Sawyer
I gotta right

I gotta right, you gotta right, we all gotta right to the Tree of Life

elisions and the insertion of the extra beat syllable. They can change 'The Blood came trickling down' into the magic of 'The Blood came a-twinklin' down', or 'I have done what you told me to do' into 'I done done-a what ya tol' me to do.'

Their poetry and songs, secular and religious, show that the early African slaves in America had the creativeness, adaptability and understanding reflected in their tribal visual arts, yet they produced no surviving art during the colonial period. There could have been few craft artists among them, for the importance of good craftsmen generally kept them safely at home; and the few could scarcely function without the patronage and compelling tribal needs to which they were accustomed. After the War of Independence new situations matured which encouraged American Negroes, slave and free, to make art. It could not be an Africanized art, though there were hints of the tribal past in it, and it was made for masters and not their own people, but it was art.

THE SPONSORING YEARS

Culturally, colonial America was a desert with few oases. It could not be watered from England; and there was little water for the arts in a way of life which dismissed the painter as one 'who draws only to please the Eye'. The 'curious Carver' was worse, for he employed 'his art to please the Fancy', instead of being content, like the honest carpenter, to devote his skill to 'more serviceable' ends.

Poets, when Shakespeare, Marvell and their roistering successors of the Restoration were within living experience, produced regional mounds of trite versification that make one almost indulgent towards the horrors of Anglo-Indian poesy. In the north they had the proportions of mass; elsewhere they amounted altogether to an ant-hill; and from Maine to the outposts the poetic insensibility of

Robert Blackburn
The Toiler

*Harmon
Foundation*

people to whom the noble Psalms of Miles Coverdale belonged by inheritance was emphasized by the almost incredible atrocities of the *Bay Psalm Book* of 1640.

But other circumstances, and the not negligible feeling of a promise to the future, required the remaking of America's social organization; and the infirmities of imperium, brandishing customary faith in ordained power and the determination to apply it, hastened what was inevitable. The Stamp Act of 1765 forced the turning point. The extent to which it influenced tempers and sharpened wits is illuminated by an exceptionally prophetic warning in the *Court Miscellany* for 1769: 'Remarks, which are supposed will be made in this Kingdom, by two North American travellers in the year 1944' by *Rationalis*.

It visualizes London in ruins through bombing and America as the foremost imperial nation, 'which now gives law to so many regions', though they 'were once subject colonies, who being treated more like aliens than fellow subjects, caused great disturbance, which ended in your ruin and their imperial grandeur. For, whilst the important matter of right was in dispute, and the now imperial Americans were remonstrating, your ministers were running horses at Newmarket. These, with many other acts of dissipation, intemperance, injustice, violence, ignorance, and despotism, are the true cause of your present forlorn and wretched condition'.

Seven years later the Declaration of Independence was proclaimed. Critics have admired its 'sonorous prose', while noting its 'factual inaccuracies' and ideological borrowings from John Locke and others; but the man who wrote it knew its sources were beyond booksy analysis, for he insisted that it was 'an expression of the American mind'.

Understandably, the American mind at that time shared the still persistent governing conceit crystallized in a limerick I owe to an unusual British scientist, the late Professor Frederic Wood Jones, FRS:

Most folk who have the gene for 'pink behind'
Hold a belief that seems a trifle odd:
They fancy they alone of all mankind
Are fashioned in the form of God.

Therefore, freedom meant democratic self-government, 'Life, Liberty and the pursuit of Happiness' being the 'inalienable Rights' of those who possessed the gene. Indians were too naughty and unappreciative to share these divine endowments: they deserved extermination in the interests of expansion and prosperity. Negroes were too stupid and immoral, if they were human at all, to be included: the public weal demanded that they should not be spared the rod, except on Sundays.

But the greater truth is that after the Declaration America, and the world, could never be the same again. There were democrats, as humble as Paine and aristocratic as Jefferson, who tirelessly nourished the new hopes for all mankind in this fertilizing document. Their many successes included regional prohibitions against the slave trade which culminated in its total abolition throughout the United States in 1808, slavery itself being abolished in the northern states three years earlier. The crowning of cotton as king limited this achievement, but slavery was doomed when America became free.

Moreover, the humanists of the day knew that the effective abolition of social evils requires conditions in which goodness can flourish. They realized that the future of the republic depended on a culture rooted in the land.

So it was that the first real poet, and by that fact the first real artist, of America was not a seeker of the muse, but an active abolitionist, Philip Morin Freneau (1752–1832), who served his purposes by being editor of the *National Gazette*, writer, government official, trader, farmer, sailor and captain of a privateer during the revolutionary war. He hated because he loved. His tone ranges from caricature and fang-toothed invective to tender and imaginative lyrics of man and nature. He gave America its own Romantic vision; and he painted into its literature and art the landscapes we know so well:

Pale ivy round him grew, and mingled vines,
Plantains, bananas ripe, and yellow pines.

In fact, creative humanism in America began with Freneau, but he was more than a pioneer. He was a man of his time, whose work reflected the character and pace of artistic productivity during the first years of free America. His contemporaries added a library of poetry, not much of it outstanding, but most of it lively and interesting.

The American scene remained, as Thomas Moore wrote in 1804, 'betwixt half-polish'd and half-barbarous life', but it was certainly not 'one dull chaos'—the mind that made *Lalla Rookh* was obviously not equipped for penetrating social criticism. A country beset by external threats, torn by internal conflicts and inherited contradictions, hell bent on territorial expansion, and surging with a multiplicity of needs, could scarcely be called dull.

Nor could it be called chaotic if we remember that growth is proliferation. Some, at least, of the uglinesses of the past were being cleared away. The great feudal estates were breaking down and new lands,

James Wells   *Street Scene*

I scattered seed enough to plant the land
In rows from Canada to Mexico
But for my reaping only what the hand
Can hold at once is all that I can show
                                        Arna Bontemps

often unfortunately, were there for the taking. Agriculture, though suffering from the still universal lunacy of concentration on cash crops, was flourishing. Commerce, industry and banking were moving to the frontiers and across the seas. Schools, colleges and institutions were increasing spectacularly.

Consequently, before Freneau died, the country which was so intensely his country had gone a long way towards becoming a new land with new people —immigrants who brought new skills and ideas, and a new generation of prospering natives who sensed that men and nations do not live by bread and dollars alone. They wanted beauty so much that the carver, no longer 'curious', became a craftsman whose work was sought everywhere for ships, shops, churches, public buildings, homes and gardens.

In these circumstances artists no longer depended on flattering grandees. They had faith in the people. Charles Winslow Peale could add a brood, confidently named Raphaelle, Rembrandt, Rubens, Titian, Angelica Kauffman, Franklin and Linnaeus, to the group so delightfully portrayed in *The Peale Family* because he knew that 'people have a growing taste for the arts, and are becoming more and more fond of encouraging their progress amongst them'.

Indeed, the taste was growing so fast that the discovery of Negro talents was inevitable. The hands that hoed the fields could make many things, useful and beautiful; and the increasing inclination was to encourage them to add decoration to utility. The Negroes made the most beautiful things they could; and those things are the beginnings of art by American Negroes. It is American art, but it is also Negro art. For Negroes are Americans—and Negroes.

15

THE MANUAL ARTS

History offers no date for the beginnings of art by American Negroes: it never does for any art. But, since people and peoples like to push the origins of their cultures as far back as possible, it will be agreeable to assume that chosen Negroes were craftsmen during the early days of colonial America. They must have made many of the things needed in the home and now and then they probably made something very good; but the things needed, like the homes themselves (which they helped to build), were rough and too uncherished to survive.

The situation was different after the mid-eighteenth century. Increasing prosperity, education, comfort and good taste promoted a greater variety of needs; and favoured slaves, not infrequently raised on the plantations with the biological assistance of Massa himself, were trained to meet them. The larger plantations often had their own smithies, workshops and tanneries; the smaller establishments found it expedient on occasions to rent talented slaves to local craftsmen; and quite a few owners took creative pleasure in securing the addition of aesthetic appeal to utility.

Sometimes master and slave were both craftsmen. The following advertisement, for example, is said by James Porter (1943) to 'be typical of the printed records', especially with reference to ironwork:

> To Planters. A white workman, blacksmith by trade, who own a negro slave also a blacksmith (and he has no other dependents) wants employment upon a plantation where a smithy is already established or whose owner wishes to establish one. Address in the city (New Orleans) Mr A. Bonamy. October 6 (1809)

Besides, the numbers of free Negro artisans, urged by inclination and circumstances to make their products attractive as well as useful, were increasing rapidly. Indicative figures are the rise of 'free people of colour' from 59,557 in 1790 (nearly 9 per cent. of the total Negro population in the United States) to 488,070 in 1860, or nearly 11 per cent. of the Negro population of 4,441,830. These free Negroes, of whom a third were mulattoes in 1850, were landowners (in 1840 some 4,000 were slaveowners too) as well as professional men, merchants, tradesmen, artisans and semi-skilled labourers. Only a fraction were unskilled labourers as the price of freedom was high.

The pride of the good workman should, of course, be added to the complex of major causes which promoted artistic craftsmanship amongst Negroes. J. W. C. Pennington, who endured slavery until his father was cruelly treated, published a book in 1850 in which he said (quoted from E. Franklin Frazier):

> I had always aimed to be trustworthy; and feeling a high degree of mechanical pride, I had aimed to do my work with dispatch and skill; my blacksmith's pride and trade was one thing that had reconciled me so long to remain a slave. I sought to distinguish myself in the finer branches of the business by invention and finish; I frequently tried my hand at making guns and pistols, putting blades in pen knives, making fancy hammers, hatchets, sword-cases, &c., &c. . . .

The conditions favouring the making of art on a regional scale were nowhere better in early America than in Louisiana, though it was afflicted by the rivalries of the major European powers. Its history begins with the coming of the French to the Gulf of Mexico in 1699, when they founded a settlement at Biloxi on the Mississippi Sound. Spreading to the head of the Mississippi Delta, they established the town of New Orleans in 1718; but in 1763 the Treaty of Paris compelled them to relinquish its administration, and that of the colony centred on it, to Spain, which surrendered Florida, where it had built the colony of St Augustine in 1565, to the British. Napoleon, who got Louisiana back in 1802, sold it to the United States; and in 1812 it became a State.

It has remained an interestingly different State, though Oliver Larkin assures us that 'History had reserved the future for men and women who could become individuals and who could mold their own lives and institutions.' Advance bookings, we gather, were denied to the French and Spanish in America because the former 'did not adapt themselves to frontier realities' and the latter 'assimilated the native peoples'. Apart from the fact that it was the Spaniards who were assimilated, English supremacy in colonial America depended on successes in European wars rather than special mental qualities, 'racial' exclusiveness, and the favouritism of history. It must be said, too, that all men and women everywhere are individuals whose lives and institutions are moulded by interwoven factors which include their own contributions to the shaping of their societies. A gift for phrase-making should not obscure the truth that history offers no reserved seats, even to the Great Race. We make history.

Louisiana made a special kind of Gallic-flavoured history because the French, and their Spanish successors, adapted themselves so closely to 'frontier realities' that they made an agreeable way of life in the process. Pleasure, controlled by good taste and tradition, was cultivated; and wealth was generally used, in the aristocratic manner, to promote enjoyment rather than the cautious expansion of more wealth. The bounty of the Mississippi, which brought to New Orleans the abundance of the most fruitful lands in the United States, made this attitude possible.

The chief beneficiaries of Old Man River built extravagant homes rivalling the great 'West India mansions' of England. One of the earliest, *Montplaisir*, built by the Chevalier de Pradel in 1750, is described as follows by G. C. H. Kernion (quoted by Lyle Saxon):

The plans provided for a main building one hundred and six feet long by forty-eight feet wide, with wide galleries whose flooring was covered with cloth, running about its four sides. It had a gabled roof and wide attic, and contained a large dining-room, parlor, numerous bedrooms, study, laundry, and a room provided with large kettles known as the wax room, where the fruit of the *ciriers* or wax trees that grew on the place was heated in order to extract therefrom wax with which the Chevalier manufactured the candles which he later exported to France or sold in the colony. The main house, whose every window was glassed, was elevated from the ground, and leading to the main entrance was an imposing flight of steps which gave the edifice an imposing appearance. *Montplaisir* must have been truly a marvel for its day, not only on account of its architecture but also on account of its interior decorations and the beauty of the furniture that embellished it . . . its wide expanse dotted with indigo, rice, corn and vegetables, with productive orchards, with innumerable *ciriers*, and with a sawmill and a brick yard, contributed materially to defraying the Chevalier's enormous expenses.

Later, there were many comparable mansions and some that were still more magnificent and self-sufficing. The *Refinery*, built by Valcour Aimé, a sugar king, on the Mississippi between Donaldson-ville and New Orleans, was amongst the most splendid of these carefully planned mansions. Otherwise known as *Le Petit Versailles*, because its formal gardens were inspired by those of the Palace of Versailles, it was as famous for its unique hospitality as it was for its magnificence. Lyle Saxon records an occasion when an epicure's dinner, served in its marble dining hall, came entirely from Valcour Aimé's estate. It included terrapin, shrimp, crab, snipe, quail, breasts of wild duck, vegetables, salads, fruits, nuts, wines, coffee, cigars and a liqueur.

Ceremonial entertainments at *Le Petit Versailles* and elsewhere were frequently staged with Roman prodigality. When, for example, Charles Duralde celebrated the simultaneous weddings of two of his daughters at *Pine Alley*, his fabulous home in St

Martinsville, the festivities, in which 2,000 guests participated, lasted for several days. The marriage procession walked along a richly carpeted pine avenue, festooned with spiders' webs glittering with gold and silver dust, to the resplendent altar erected in front of the house. The industrious spiders were not locally caught and released along the avenue: they were imported from China.

Negroes, slave and free, supplied the enormous manpower required for building and maintaining such homes, often with quite remarkable ability. Lyle Saxon, to whom I owe my first fascinating introduction to New Orleans before the War, cites *Harvey Castle* near New Orleans as an example. Influenced by Sir Walter Scott, as many buildings of the day were, it was a three-storied, high-ceilinged mansion of thirty rooms, with two observation turrets for uninterrupted enjoyment of the surrounding scenery, built entirely by free Negroes within ninety days.

Harvey Castle was demolished in 1924, but some older houses built by Negro labour still survive. Among them *Parlange*, to the north of Baton Rouge near New Roads, has been preserved as a national monument to the Old South. Lyle Saxon's brief description of it cannot be bettered:

On either side of the driveway are octagonal brick *pigeonniers*, and the house, approached through a grove of live-oaks and pecans, is a white, green-shuttered, one-and-a-half-story raised cottage of cypress, mud and moss construction. The furnishings include rarities in silver, glass and porcelain, and many fine pieces of old furniture. The slave-made implements with which the house was built have been preserved.

Parlange (1750) is not the oldest surviving building in the Mississippi Valley. That honour belongs to the elaborate convent, rich in political and church history, first occupied by the Ursuline nuns of New Orleans in 1734. Slave responsibility for its construction extended to forging its metalwork.

After its disastrous fires of 1788 and 1795, the rapid building of New Orleans relied on skilled and unskilled Negro labour. Good taste and good workmanship secured the lasting Spanish-French distinction of the buildings, remarkable for their wrought iron balconies, doors, grilles, lamp standards and other ornaments, of the Vieux Carré and elsewhere. Their graceful wrought iron (very different from the later cast iron, Teutonically heavy with oak and grapevine motifs, of the Philadelphia foundries) derived its patterns from Baroque, Rococo and Neo-classic models, but they were integrated, with an added touch of Gothic, in a manner that is distinctly and delightfully local.

The discovery that the wrought iron of New Orleans represented an 'American art' naturally caused much excitement in the 'twenties. The tone was set by a highly flavoured article in *The New York Times Magazine* (8 August 1926) which declared in its title that the 'Negro's Art Lives in His Wrought Iron'. The writer (H.B.L.) was convinced that 'It is solid and tangible proof that the negro brought with him into his slavery the ancient art tendencies of Africa.' The same opinion was more strongly expressed by James Porter, usually cautious, in 1958:

> The wrought iron balconies of the Old Quarter of New Orleans and of certain houses of Mobile, Alabama, and even of Charleston, South Carolina, have been shown to be proofs of the survival of skills in woodcrafts and metallurgy brought by the African from the land of his birth. There was a type of 'plantation' pottery produced by slave craftsmen that bore the unmistakable marks of African influence in the distinguishing peculiarities of surface design.

Actually, proofs of the extent to which Negroes participated in forging the wrought iron of the Deep South are circumstantial rather than documentary; and it is stretching the evidence to call it a 'Negro art' arising from an African heritage. 'Africanism' is rare even in American Negro woodcraft, though the material itself facilitates the continuity of decorative treatment from one generation to another—the walking stick carved in 1863 by Henry Gudgell, a slave in Missouri, is the only example (plate 6) we have been able to find from the continental United States. The interesting pottery to which Mr Porter refers is no more than the descriptive phrase 'slave pottery' implies. Its purposes, inspiration and making are wholly American. A token of growing group consciousness, its Negroness is the Negroness of the Southern States, not Africa.

The fact is that crafts meet needs—and the artisan slaves mostly met the needs of their masters. For this reason alone we can assume that Negroes were considerably employed in hammering out iron implements, supports and ornaments. Additional arguments are the myth that blacks are better able to stand high temperatures than whites; that they were trained for work in the plantation smithies; and that, towards the end of the eighteenth century, Negroes were dominant throughout the South in the production of plain and ornamental iron. In skilled labour generally 100,000 out of the 120,000 Southern 'mechanics' in 1865 were Negroes. The high capacity for creative adjustment indicated by this situation, and by the scale on which Negroes were integrated into all forms of early American production, seems to be more important to Negro morale than exaggerations about the inheritance of 'ancestral skills'.

The flowering of wrought iron in the Deep South ended with increased immigration, the advance of industry, and the proliferating Doric columns of the Greek Revival. For no architectural good reason at all, *Oak Alley* (1836) near Donaldsonville, one of the show places of Louisiana, is segmented by twenty-eight such pillars, each eight feet around; and to emphasize the feeling of enduring greatness which they are intended to give they are matched by twenty-eight more than correspondingly massive oaks.

Negroes, all over the South, helped to build, supply and service such homes, as well as the larger number of lesser proportions. Their skills provided the innumerable needs in iron, wood, leather, clay, fibres, fabrics and textiles of the plantation, farm and home, while their ability in the kitchen and at the table maintained the reputation for hospitality enjoyed by so many colonels and their ladies.

Some of the things they made are illustrated in this book through the enthusiastic generosity of the Index of American Design. Others are represented in the great picture-collection of the Index and many, in regional museums and private homes, await discovery. We would have liked, for example, to have shown a work by Thomas Day of Charleston, South Carolina, a leading Negro cabinetmaker in the mid-nineteenth century; but Helen McCormack, Director of the Gibbes Art Gallery, Charleston, S.C., could not even locate him, though her determined efforts included searching through the local directories from 1818 to 1870.

Miss McCormack did, however, note that Negro cabinetmakers were successful in the region, for five were listed in the directory for 1869–70; and, with references to Negro silversmiths before 1800, she added a tantalizing quotation from a paper by Anna Wells Rutledge (1949) about 'Ned, the carver':

> In 1859 the *Mercury* announced 'a new and handsome hearse. . . . The sides are ornamented by carving in wood, representing the weeping willow, encircled by appropriate drapery, surmounting which is an urn, and underneath a quiver—all emblematical of the purpose for which the vehicle is intended. This carving was executed by an humble coloured man named Ned, belonging to Mr Brown, and would be no discredit to an artist of greater pretensions.'

Unfortunately, Miss McCormack could find no more about Ned or his 'new and handsome hearse'; and the quotation remains another promise of the exciting discoveries which await serious research on the manual arts of the American Negro people.

TOWARDS FREEDOM AND ART

The benefits gained by American Negroes from advancing needs scarcely mitigated the essential inhumanity of slavery, nor did they prove that 'Never was talent and flair more scientifically turned into specialization'. In fact, horrors multiplied as the Cotton Empire expanded and 'philosophers' justified its slave economy by the peculiar fitness of the Negro for absolute servitude. The renewal of the African slave trade, it was thought, 'would be a blessing to the American people, and a benefit to the African himself'.

The expansion was so rapid that 6 million bales of cotton were exported in 1860 against half a million in 1820, the resulting demand for 'hands' being reflected in the rise of the slave population from 697,624 in 1790 to 4 million in 1860. Their value as property, estimated at 3,000 million dollars, crushed Abraham Lincoln when he drafted and signed the historic Proclamation of Emancipation (1 January 1863). He muttered as he took up his pen: 'It must be done. I am driven to it.'

It follows that slaves were illegally imported in more than thousands long after 1808, but the phenomenal increase in slave labour can mostly be accounted for by high fertility and breeding on a commercial scale. Moncure Conway, a pioneer humanist, noted that 'the chief pecuniary resource in the border states is the breeding of slaves' and there is much support for this statement in plantation and other records. Consequently, the internal trade was so brisk that it was strongly competitive:

> Negroes for Sale. Just arrived with a large lot of Virginia and Maryland Negroes, which I offer cheap at my old stand, corner of Esplanade and Chartres Streets (New Orleans), and will be receiving fresh lots every month during the season. Call and see me before you purchase elsewhere. Joseph Bruin.

Yet very few people owned slaves. Three-quarters of the southern whites managed to exist without them and most of the rest owned less than five. Wealth was stored in the coffers of a small 'plantocracy', but almost every southern white had a vested interest, fortified by racial conceits, in the perpetuation of slavery.

In the North a different viewpoint prevailed. There, and in industrial England, the slave economy was regarded as a threat to the growth of free trade capitalism based on wage labour. Besides, just as the planters had to find more land by territorial expansion, industry had to find more markets; and it was clear that if the slaves could become consumers, instead of being only producers, they would provide a handsome market no matter how humbly they consumed. Abolitionist sentiments fitted nicely into the new economics.

The feudal South could not resist this combination of enlightened capitalism, industrial power and morality; but the North could not rescue the freed slaves from the aftermath of poverty, resentment and Yankee practices in the South. The slaves became, for the most part, landless peasants or unskilled wage labourers, who suffered increasingly from exploitation, segregation and the oppressions of a lynching, shotgun régime. They stepped from the outhouse into the ghetto.

But even a mean freedom is better than none; and the Negroes, taking every opportunity offered, soon justified hopes in their potentialities as consumers. Today, though their average income is one-third that of the white, the purchasing power of America's 15 million Negroes is estimated at well over 15,000 million dollars a year. Approximately the value of the annual export trade of the United States, it equals the purchasing power of Canada, and exceeds that of Latin America. This significant fact, coupled with the Negro vote, the economic wastefulness of segregation, and the influence of international opinion, explains the slow but definite improvement in attitudes towards American Negroes. It also helps to explain, if we remember that it is a stage in progress, the cultural advance from making art for masters or patrons to making art because one must.

Free mulattoes in the South fostered this advance extensively, for they formed a relatively privileged group, with a fair-skinned élite, which was more admired than hated. They were nowhere better off than in Louisiana, where the permissiveness that comes from sensuality was kept at peak by the irresistible quadroon girls. These girls could not marry whites, as equal political and social rights were not allowed to 'free persons of colour', but they made it extremely difficult for whites to emphasize their superior status. Many were so fair that it would have been dangerous to act against them on a suspicion of *café au lait*, while some had the additional security of fathers or lovers who were men of high importance.

The semi-privileged status of this group of mulattoes in the early nineteenth century is admiringly described by Charles Gayarré in Grace King's book on *New Orleans*:

> By 1830, some of these *gens de couleur* had arrived at such a degree of wealth as to own cotton and sugar plantations with numerous slaves. They educated their children, as they had been educated,

in France. Those who chose to remain there, attained, many of them, distinction in scientific and literary circles. In New Orleans they became musicians, merchants, and money and real estate brokers. The humbler classes were mechanics; they monopolised the trade of shoemakers . . .; they were barbers, tailors, carpenters, upholsterers. They were notably successful hunters and supplied the city with game. As tailors, they were almost exclusively patronised by the élite, so much so that the Legoasters', the Dumas', the Clovis', and Lacroix', acquired individually fortunes of several hundreds of thousands of dollars. This class was most respectable; they generally married women of their own status, and led lives quiet, dignified and worthy, in homes of ease and comfort . . . they did not assume that creeping posture of debasement—nor did the whites expect it—which has more or less been forced upon them in fiction.

Clarence Laughlin's superb photographs and scholarly familiarity with old Louisiana allow us to look at and into one of these 'homes of ease and comfort'—*Melrose*, originally *Yucca*, on the Cane River near Natchitoches. It began about 1750 as a

home (plate 2), constructed by packing a mixture of earth, deer-hair and moss between cypress planks, for Marie Thérèse, a slave freed by the French commandant of the fort in Natchitoches. There is probably no older dwelling in the United States built by Negroes for a Negro; and it is also one of the earliest surviving buildings in the South. It should be a national museum.

Contemporary with it is the unique 'African House' (plate 3) nearby. A solid structure of brick and timber, divided on the ground floor into a commissary and a prison, it simplified the control of the fifty-eight slaves who worked the 2,000 acres owned by Marie Thérèse and her Parisian husband, Thomas Metoyer.

The original home of the Metoyers sufficed the family until 1833, when their grandson, Louis Metoyer, built the present main house (to which the wings were added in 1904) of the plantation. At that time the mulatto community of Louisiana, unable to cope with the rising tide of Americanism, was already on the way to less prosperous days; and in 1847 *Melrose* was no longer a mulatto house. That

Margaret Burroughs
Sojourner Truth

Charles White
John Brown

Courtesy
Atlanta Univ.

Two Great Fighters for Freedom

20

its Metoyer history has been preserved is a tribute to those who have lived in it since then.

Before the main house was built, Augustine Metoyer, the eldest son of Thomas and Marie, transformed the accommodation he had inherited: the living room (plate 2), one of two main rooms in what remained a modest cabin, has a quite surprising distinction. Dominating it is the large portrait of Augustine by Feuville (1829), evidently painted to commemorate, as we gather from his indicating hand, the completion in 1829 of St. Augustine's Church. It was meant to be his most lasting gift to the community he served as a leader.

The adjacent portraits, unsigned and undated, are those of his wife and daughter (see also plate 4), to which Mr Laughlin's generous co-operation has allowed us to add an unsigned portrait (plate 4) of one of Marie Metoyer's grandsons, probably Louis. Who are these portraits by, and who was Feuville? The questions should tease a Negro art historian into seeking the answers.

Meanwhile, the indications are that there were several portrait painters amongst the mulattoes of Louisiana, especially New Orleans, in the early nineteenth century. So far only one, Julien Hudson, is known by his pictures—a fascinating self-portrait made more remarkable by an ample nose which qualifies him, in this respect, as a lesser Cyrano de Bergerac amongst Negroes; and a sympathetic portrait (plate 8) which reveals Colonel Jean Michel Fortier Jr (1774–1836), Commander of the Corps of Free Men of Colour in the victorious Battle of New Orleans (1815), as the sensitive, cultured and gallant gentleman he was.

The Metoyer portraits, combined with the importance attached to painted likenesses in oils by those who are intent on building family traditions, promise an interesting chapter in the early history of American Negro art when the portraits owned by old Negro families are sought and studied. We can assume, too, since family traditions cannot be built unless families identify themselves with a rising group, that the free Negroes had reached a high level of organized independence in Augustine Metoyer's day; and the initial stages of independence are always characterized by a cultural upsurge which produces more portraits—at first of the famous and then of the folk as well. This situation remains striking today.

It began with a trend towards religious separatism during and after the War of Independence. The white churches could not implement the doctrinal position that slavery was contrary to Divine laws by accepting Negroes as equals, for that would have been prejudicial to slavery, particularly as 'trouble-making' Negro ministers would have had to be ordained.

Charles White
There were no crops this year
Courtesy Barnett Aden Gallery

They stepped from the outhouse into the ghetto

Consequently, when the American churches reflected the temper of the new State by establishing their autonomy, Negro Christians followed their example by founding their own religious organizations. A Negro Baptist Church was built near Augusta, Georgia, in 1773 and another in Petersburg, Virginia, in 1776; and by the turn of the century several Baptist and Methodist churches were ministering exclusively to the needs of coloured people.

In the North, where religious and political instruction could be more fearlessly combined, several leaders emerged whose churches were centres of vigorous agitation. Richard Allen was one of the most remarkable of these patriots. A precocious and determined youth, he bought himself out of slavery when he was seventeen or so and soon began to earn

21

John Biggers
Cradle

*Courtesy Houston
Museum of Fine Arts*

a Young African Painter, on Seeing His Works'; but the works she mentions are allegorical. The portrait frontispiece to her *Poems* (1773) may have been engraved by him—or by Sarah Moorhead, the artist-wife of his master.

A later bishop of the A.M.E. Church was Jermain W. Loguen (1814–1871). A fugitive slave, a fearless opponent of the Fugitive Slave Act of 1850, a tireless leader of the Underground Railroad (the organization which aided escaping slaves), a fighting soldier in Canada in 1838, and a minister in Syracuse, New York, who found trouble when he was not in it, his personality and experiences should reward a lively biographer. The depth and appeal of his handsome, confident, sensitive, somewhat sensual, good-humoured face, is happily caught in his portrait (plate 8) by William Simpson.

Simpson also recorded the compassionate, deter-

a reputation as a preacher. He believed that 'our forlorn and deplorable situation earnestly and loudly demands of us to devise and pursue all legal means for the speedy elevation of ourselves and brethren to the scale and standing of men'; and he followed his convictions by founding the Free African Society, actively sponsoring the first national Negro convention, associating himself with other progressive movements, and establishing (1794) the Bethel African Methodist Episcopal church in Philadelphia. Its many branches grouped themselves in 1816 into a formal religious organization, with Allen as its first duly consecrated bishop, known as the African Methodist Episcopal Church. No other Methodist body has as many Negro members today.

Educational and cultural activities were among the earliest concerns of the A.M.E. churches and it is accordingly fitting that the first portrait of a Negro by a Negro, in so far as we know at present, is a charming pastel (plate 8) of Richard Allen at the age of twenty-five. It was drawn in 1785 and James Porter, who is almost certainly right, suggests that it is the work of G. W. Hobbs, then a minister in Baltimore. He had, writes Mr Porter, 'virtually established himself as the portrait painter of the Methodist Episcopal church in that area', but his works await discovery.

Scipio Moorhead of Boston was painting before 1773, as we know from a poem by Phillis Wheatley, the first Negro to write conventional verse, 'To S.M.,

John Biggers
Mother and Child

*Courtesy
Atlanta Univ.*

High fertility is one of the reasons for the exceptional frequency of the motherhood theme in American Negro Art

22

mined, Bible-steeped expression of Loguen's good-looking colleague and wife, Caroline; but little is known about him or his works. Several other self-taught Negro portrait painters of the years before the Civil War are now obscure through inattention, though passing references to them show that they were popular.

Patrick Reason, fortunately, is relatively well known, as he was an engraver and lithographer in New York City who was actively associated with the Anti-Slavery Society. His most famous engraving, circulated throughout the world in Abolitionist publications, plaques and medals (and recently printed on the title page and page 104 of the *Pictorial History of the Negro in America* by Langston Hughes and Milton Meltzer), is that of the pleading, chained slave who asks the question 'Am I not a man and a brother?' A picture that has fulfilled its purpose so productively is above discussion in terms of art, but it should be observed that it is one of the rare early attempts at figure composition by Negro artists.

On the whole, Reason was a technically limited craftsman raised above his artistic stature by his passionate feelings about the injustices of the day: the intensity which makes some of his portraits notable is partly the reflexion of his own intensity. Typical examples are his paintings of outstanding fugitive slaves; his pencil drawing (page 81) of De Witt Clinton (1769–1828), the man of vision (he planned New York City and promoted the Erie Canal) and reforming zeal who reconciled high principles with being the father of the party patronage 'spoils system'; and his more pedestrian engrav-

John Wilson   *Courtesy*
Mother and Child   *Atlanta Univ.*

ing (plate 8) of Granville Sharp (1735–1813), the pioneer English Abolitionist.

The portraits by Reason, and by his predecessors and contemporaries, deny the statement by Dr J. Hall Pleasants that the 'first American Negro portrait painter of whom there has hitherto been a record was Robert S. Duncanson'; nor is it true that the honour belongs to Joshua Johnston. Dr Pleasants has, however, rendered a major service in identifying twenty-one canvases, recognizably by the same limner and in the best tradition of early American primitive portrait painting, attributed to Joshua Johnston and given possible dates from 1790 to 1825. Their style varies little from that of the rigidly posed, staring James McCormick family (plate 7) sitting uncomfortably on a brass-tacked Sheraton settee, though the quality and compelling personality of the *grande dame* is attractively conveyed in his portrait of Mrs John Moale (plate 7).

These pictures are also representative of the patronage Johnston enjoyed in Baltimore society, yet nothing is known about him. Dr Pleasants thinks that he was probably a free mulatto—light enough to be listed as a portrait painter, without designation of colour, in the Baltimore directories between 1796 and 1824, except that in 1817 he is included among the 'Free Householders of Colour'. The evidence enhances a mystery which should excite further inquiry.

Tom Feelings   *Courtesy C.A.G.*
Motherhood   *New York*

23

Scion of fused strength am I
All understanding
Nor this, nor that
Contains me
Georgia Douglas Johnson

Decoration by Irene Clark

MULATTOES AND ATELIER ART

In happier days, when the doctrines of the dis-established church could be read without locking the door, Christopher Caudwell observed that 'none is more unlovely' than the lower middle class. 'It has only one value in life, that of bettering itself. . . . It is rootless, individualist, lonely, and perpetually facing, with its hackles up, an antagonistic world. . . . It has no traditions of its own . . . (it) is like a terrible stagnant marsh, all mud and bitterness, and without even the saving grace of tragedy.'

Comparable convictions are expresssed in E. Franklin Frazier's arresting book on the *Black Bourgeoisie*, a group which is essentially a lower middle class. It 'is without cultural roots in either the Negro world with which it refuses to identify, or the white world which refuses to permit the black bourgeoisie to share its life'. Analysis of this premise leads to the concluding judgement that 'Gertrude Stein would have been nearer the truth if she had said of the black bourgeoisie what she said of Negroes in general, that they "were not suffering from persecution, they were suffering from nothing-ness" . . . because when Negroes attain middle-class status, their lives generally lose both content and significance'. There could scarcely be a more dis-quieting state in a community which necessarily relies heavily on this class for the making and appre-ciation of art.

The 'black bourgeoisie' began with mulattoes and is still dominated, in numbers and social condition-ing, by them. Like the Eurasians, they were always snobs, motivated by vested interests, 'getting on' and breeding themselves into a pallid aristocracy of money, property and the right skin colour. 'Although they were not white,' writes Franklin Frazier, 'they could thank God that they were not black.' They did more than that. They organized themselves against blacks. As early as 1790, they formed a Brown Fellowship Society in Charleston, South Carolina; and later The Blue Vein Circle flourished in various places in the South. Its attitudes were crystallized (or satirized?) in rhyme:

Stan' back, black man,
You cain't shine;
Yo' lips is too thick,
An' you hain't my kin'.

Stan' back, black man!
Cain't you see
Dat a kinky-headed chap
Hain't nothin' side o' me?

But they also provided the men, the means, and the standards which fostered, for better and worse, the phenomenal progress of the American Negro people from slavery to the greatest, most highly organized, coloured minority in the world today. It is a record, considered in its determining social con-text, in which both black and brown men can take pride; and if the other side of the medal seems tar-nished, they can remember with Langston Hughes that:

The past has been
A mint of blood and sorrow—
That must not be
True of tomorrow.

It follows that their rôle in the cultural develop-ment of American Negroes has been dominant, too; for in seeking status they necessarily sought culture

24

Jacob Lawrence
Ambulance Call

*Courtesy Robert Carlen, Philadelphia, from
the sales collection of the Carlen Galleries*
Specially photographed for this book

Eldzier Cortor
Trio V
Special photograph for this
book by Carl Van Vechten

as well. Critically, as Franklin Frazier has said in an early work (1939), 'their creative efforts . . . appear naïve and pitiable.' Their poetry is a collection of 'sorry imitations in stilted language and burdened with classical references'. Their numerous literary societies, 'in which the frail vines of their culture were watered', reek with 'an atmosphere of artificiality and aloofness from the real world'; and, if we are looking for fun, there 'is certainly cause for amusement' in them.

All this, and more, can be admitted. Yet, however they appear now, what is really remarkable about the cultural efforts, which reflected the prevailing culture and met community needs, of the first few generations of free mulattoes is that they were made by fundamentally underprivileged people in the midst of a slave economy. Alexis de Tocqueville, observing it in 1831, saw that it 'dishonours labour; it introduces idleness into society, and with idleness, ignorance and pride, luxury and distress. It enervates the powers of the mind, and benumbs the activity of man. The influence of slavery, united to the English character, explains the manners and the social condition of the Southern States.'

Indeed, it enervated Southern minds so much that they granted to Negroes, who were not 'people of the United States' in the sense of the Constitution, 'no rights which a white man need respect'. Coloured persons, 'whether emancipated or not', had 'no right or privileges but such as those who held the power and the government might choose to grant them'. This was the decision of the Supreme Court in 1857 on the plea of Dred Scott that he had become a free man by virtue of long residence on free soil.

The circumstances we have discussed, at the risk of being accused by the not so advanced avant garde of 'sociological digressions', explain the successes and failures of American Negro art, its wide appeal and social protest as well as its amateurishness, sentimentality and coterie affectations. The whole of this art, and the parts which might seem to be greater than the whole or not to belong to it, can be fully appreciated only in the perspectives of a peculiar social heritage—and the polarity of the mulatto rôle in making it.

The expansion of this rôle in the first five decades of the nineteenth century nourished the evolution of atelier art by American Negroes from the craftsman art we have discussed. Until after the First World War, it contributed little to the progress of their people or the advancement of American art, but it did prove that Negroes could make art according to the values and techniques of the day. Moreover, it offered a challenge to study which was invariably accepted, in spite of the difficulties involved.

Its history begins with Robert Duncanson (1817–72), who supported his early career as a painter by printing daguerreotypes, and Eugene Warbourg (1825–61), a stonemason turned sculptor. Duncanson was a Scots Canadian mulatto born in New York State, educated in Canada, and resident in Cincinnati and Detroit from 1842–59. Most of his later life was spent in Europe, where classical tradition took him to Italy and paternal tradition to Scotland: he had been there before at the expense of the Anti-Slavery League. He died, insane, at Detroit.

As an artist Duncanson was a literary Romantic, immoderately drunk on Tennyson and Scott, who missed the great days of Romanticism and lacked association with the Hudson River School which developed visual lyricism in America. As a person he can scarcely be called sympatico. James Porter, who has given him the distinction of an enthusiastic and admirably illustrated memoir in Art in America (1951), finds in his art no sign of 'the least bitterness of spirit or preoccupation with other concerns than those proper to painting and industrious self-cultivation'. But differences about the propriety of these concerns has kept the art world in a state of war for several decades, while the word for 'industrious self-cultivation' is egotism—so obsessional in Duncanson that it led to the delusion that he was 'directly inspired by the spirit of one of the great masters'.

An associated delusion, accounting for his apparent lack of bitterness, was the feeling of superiority which caused him to reject the Negro people and identify himself with Scotland. 'I am not interested in colour (problems), only paint', Hale Woodruff approvingly quotes him as saying. The statement is the essential autobiography of a character afflicted beyond recognition of the momentous struggle around him, or appreciation of the progressive attitudes of the patrons who sustained him.

Their sympathy, rather more than Duncanson's merits, gave him a certain vogue which might not otherwise have survived the clumsy and stilted triteness of his earlier attempts at genre: we show two (plate 18) as social relics. Uncle Tom is Uncle Tomish enough to have wrung the heart of any dear old lady in a crinoline, but The Drunkard's Plight has an unexpected roguish humour which reminds us of the once popular, and still pathetic, refrain 'Father, dear father, come home with me now.'

The eight years separating these two pictures seem to have added little to his competence, nor did the twelve years between his portraits of the Berthelets and that of Nicholas Longworth (plate 18), the most generous friend of artists and good causes in Ohio. All have the quality, common to white and coloured limners before him, of presenting strong characters forcefully; and all leave the impression that, with more discipline and less 'self-cultivation', Duncanson could have become a great portrait painter.

Mr Porter thinks highly of the 'painter-like values' of the lighting and props in the portrait of Nicholas Longworth: 'the artist here draws upon realism, luministic romanticism and academic neo-classicism all at once to achieve a work of sincerity and finesse.' But the masters of portraiture, however addicted to romantic vistas, never assaulted the intelligence with incongruity; and a poorly depicted figure, illuminated by a light from nowhere and standing awkwardly in the foreground of the artist's unrelated decorative fancies, is certainly incongruous. The grapes which have no business on the table, and the envelope addressed to Duncanson which lies more inexcusably at the feet of an obviously tidy man, are worked in references to Longworth's productive interest in viticulture and patronage of the artist, rather than part of a sustained symbolic treatment. Yet, by excluding these distractions, we see in the head and shoulders a masterly portrayal of brooding seriousness and responsibility.

Longworth's support deserved a more unified acknowledgement than that ridiculously placed envelope. It included the exceptional opportunity to decorate the halls of his imposing home, now the Taft Museum, in Cincinnati. The romantic landscape murals Duncanson created for it, though reminiscently British in spite of their sometimes impossible botany, are a possession of American architectural art in which pride would be warranted. For Duncanson himself they began a career as a landscape painter which quickly reached distinction in *Blue Hole*, *Flood Waters*, *Little Miami River* (plate 17). The charm, now so nostalgic, of this American idyll, was never quite repeated in his later landscapes, though some, such as *Water Hole on the Miami River* (Wilberforce University, Ohio) and *Valley Pasture* (in the Wendell P. Dabney collection at Cincinnati) have the appeal of pastoral simplicity.

Significantly, he did not repeat his American achievements in Scotland, where the weight of Sir Walter Scott's prose, lying heavily upon him, seems to have submerged his interpretations in massive gloom. Occasionally, however, he escaped from Scott with very satisfying results, as a last seascape, 'heaving, boundless, endless and sublime' (one must hope he had forgotten *Childe Harold*) in the Cincinnati Art Museum shows. The next year he was dead and so soon forgotten, Mr Porter complains, that the Cincinnati Centennial Exposition of 1880 hung no work of his in its special exhibition of art.

Eugene Warbourg, unfortunately, has not yet found a Porter, though his name has been an aside in Negro scholarship for forty years. He shared a stonemason's workshop in New Orleans with his brother Daniel, where he chiselled two works remembered by name, *Le Pêcheur* and *Le Premier Baiser*, and a sufficiency of portrait busts, religious statuary and graveyard memorials for some to survive. The prospects of discovering examples of what he did in Paris, to which prejudice drove him in 1852, and Rome, where he died at thirty-six, are also helpful.

Meanwhile, thanks to a friendly suggestion from Mildred Steinbach of the Frick Art Reference Library, New York, and the co-operation of John Melville Jennings, Director of the Virginia Historical Society, Richmond, we print the first reproduction (plate 19) of a marble by Warbourg. It is a robust portrait bust, impressively carved in the neo-classical manner, of a robust character: John Young Mason (1799–1859), the Virginian expansionist who believed that if Spain should refuse to sell Cuba 'then by every law, human and divine, we shall be justified in wresting it from Spain'. This work, probably done in Paris, where Young was American Minister in 1853, proves that Negro academic sculpture began with a worthy parent.

The next two American Negro artists, again a painter and a sculptor, are Edward Bannister (1828–1901) and Edmonia Lewis (1845–90). Bannister had a hard time as a young man, but his contacts were mostly outside the Negro community. It is said, though, that in 1867 a statement in the *New York Herald*, which denied that Negroes could make art, urged him to prove the contrary. He meant to do this, without benefit of patronage (he refused offers to study abroad), or emphasis on what are so absurdly called 'racial themes'. The larger truth is that Bannister, who looked like Tennyson and had an idealistic poet's view of life, was moved by a deeply rooted love for woods and waters of which landscape painting was a part; and for this reason, more than any other, he became the first Negro to earn recognition as an American regional painter of consequence. He is remembered, too, as one of the founders of the famous Providence Art Club, the fertilizing body of the Rhode Island School of Design.

Contemporary opinion rated him high. The catalogue of 101 paintings shown in the memorial exhibition arranged by the Club in 1901 contained the judgement that 'Had his nature been more self-reliant and adventurous, and had early opportunity been more kind, he might easily have been one of America's greatest landscape painters. . . .' And George W. Whitaker, writing in the *Providence Magazine* for February 1914, thought 'His paintings were poems of an elevating tendency'.

These quotations came from an affectionately esteemed artist, William Alden Brown, who has collected Bannister's pictures for over sixty years and has consistently kept his friend's name bright. Mr Brown also sent the reminiscent biographical note on Bannister—a previously unpublished contribution to Negro art history—which follows:

Edward M. Bannister was born at St. Andrews, New Brunswick, in November, 1828. His father came from the Barbadoes and his mother, Hannah Alexander, was a native of St. Andrews. At ten years of age, Bannister gave as much of his time as possible to sketching. While yet a young man, he shipped as cook on a coaster. This early experience gave him a liking for the sea. Later, he spent much time in sailing his yacht in Narragansett Bay and Newport Harbor. Time spent in yachting was not wholly time lost at painting, for George W. Whitaker tells of Bannister's continual study of skies and clouds during these days on the water.

Early in his career, he settled in Boston where he studied artistic anatomy under the famous artist and lecturer, Dr. William Rimmer. Bannister spent some time in making and enlarging solar prints, but soon entered seriously on his life work.

His first great success was in 1876, at the Centennial Exhibition in Philadelphia, where his large landscape, *Under the Oaks*, was awarded a medal of the first class. This painting sold in Boston for $1500, which at that time was considered a high price for a work by a living American artist.

For a time, honors and commissions came rapidly. He won at least three more medals.

About 1855, he married Madame Christiana Carteaux of Rhode Island South County, who was of Narragansett Indian descent. He shared a studio in Boston with Edwin Lord Weeks but came to Providence in 1871. (In a letter Mr Brown adds: I have always thought that Bannister's removal from Boston was unwise; and I have always believed that his intense interest in yachting decided him to come to Providence—Narragansett Bay is a yachtsman's paradise. . . . In the winter he spent much time ice skating on the lakes of our beautiful Roger Williams Park.)

As a boy, I visited Bannister's studio in the old Woods Buildings where later I was to become his pupil. On my first visit to the studio, Bannister moved an easel covered with drapery out from the gloomy depths at the rear of the studio. He wished my mother to see his large canvas of *Christ in the Garden of Gethsemane*, a canvas on which he worked intermittently for years. Both Mr Bannister and his wife were honored members of the Elmwood Avenue Baptist Church where my parents belonged. So at church and on Saturdays in his studio, I saw much of Bannister. His was a mind far above the ordinary and his art was in keeping with his brilliant mind. He was thoroughly conversant with the Bible, Shakespeare, English literature, classic themes and mythology.

He was one of the three so-called founding members of the Providence Art Club. On February 12, 1878, George W. Whitaker suggested to Bannister that the time was ripe for founding a club devoted to the arts. Very soon, Bannister and Whitaker took into their confidence the twenty year old artist, Charles Walter Stetson.

This trio met several times in Bannister's studio. No records of these informal meetings were kept but the interest grew and, in response to an invitation from the founding trio, a meeting was held on February 19, 1880, attended by sixteen artists, in the studio of Eimrich Rein, where the Providence Art Club came into existence. We are indebted to George L. Miner for a fine chapter in *Angell's Lane* in which the Club's founding is accurately and interestingly described.

Bannister died at a Thursday evening prayer meeting at his church in 1901.

Mr Alden Brown's insistence that 'Bannister *should* be definitely recognized as a rarely gifted painter of his period' prompted a considerable search for *Under the Oaks*, but we can only offer, along with two minor pieces, two landscapes (plates 20, 21) which local critics (and Mr Brown) have long regarded as among Bannister's best. More than regional documents of American charm in an age that has passed, they remind us, poetically and competently, that the enjoyment and communication of natural beauty is still among the proper functions of art.

Edmonia Lewis knew little of country pleasures. Orphaned early, she somehow found Abolitionist support for a short spell of schooling at Oberlin College, Ohio. She left at fifteen when accused of poisoning two of her white schoolmates. With more gaps in the story, we find her later in Boston, where she obtained some hints on modelling from a well-known sculptor, Edmund Brackett. With this encouragement, and eight dollars, she opened her own studio.

She was now an attractive young woman of East Indian appearance—many Negroes of part Amerindian origin (her mother was a Chippewa) have their twins in Asia and Southern Europe. She had, too, an appealing intensity and forthrightness, heightened by an uncultivated voice, and a tell-tale boyishness increasingly emphasized by clothes reminiscent of the more unfeminine feminists of the period.

Above all she was alight with the surety of success and the certainty that what she wrought belonged to the great struggle for freedom and beauty surrounding her. A letter rescued by James Porter stresses her sentiments. 'I will not take anything for my labor,' she writes from Rome on 5 February 1867, with reference to the emancipation group, *Forever Free*, on which she was working. 'Mr Garrison has given his whole life for my father's people and I think that I should give him a few months' work.'

Her exhibited sculpture shows this feeling from the first: it began with a medallion of John Brown and a bust of Colonel Robert Gould Shaw shown at the Boston Fair for the Soldiers' Fund in 1864. John Brown had been hanged on 2 December 1859 for an admitted 'design on my part to free slaves'. Shaw had died leading the Fifty-fourth Massachusetts Infantry, the first all-Negro regiment formed during the Civil War, in the impossible attack on Fort Wagner, Morris Island, South Carolina; and only six weeks earlier (28 May 1863) Edmonia had seen him, young, handsome and well-horsed, proudly at the head of a ceremonial parade. It would be nice if we could twist history into letting her overhear his mother whisper: 'What have I done that God has been so good to me?'

Inevitably, Mrs Shaw bought the bust, of which a further hundred copies were quickly sold. The proceeds, and the right kind of help from the Story family, took her to Rome before she was twenty—William Wetmore Story (1819–95), lawyer turned poet and sculptor, was the doge of the New England expatriates there. The dark brown boyish girl must have intrigued many of the guests at his Palazzo Barberini.

Story taught modelling to select pupils (Robert Browning was one of them), but Edmonia found a teacher and friend in Harriet Hosmer (1830–1908), a pupil of John Gibson's with the added disability of conducting a school of sculpture in a room in which Canova himself had worked. The group around Miss Hosmer showed, writes Van Wyck Brooks in *The Flowering of New England*, 'what will can do, if little else. Eager workers all, . . . they turned out busts and heroic groups, statues of American statesmen, histories in granite and romances in marble. . . . These story-telling figures possessed every accessory and association that spoke for literature as it spoke for learning and uttered an occasional word for sculpture.'

Meanwhile, from Florence, Hiram Powers (1805–73) had prepared an acquisitive market for these neo-classic exercises. Most of his 150 portrait busts, six portrait statues, and several idealizations in marble, were already circulating in their originals and copies; and his high-breasted *Greek Slave*, decoratively chained as a more symbolic substitute for the oddly placed fig leaf, was the most famous contemporary statue in the world. Victorian gentlemen could enjoy its charms in the presence of their ladies, who knew the comparisons it stimulated, but agreed to be moved by its appeal to the conscience and its condemnation of the infidel nature of the beastly 'infidel Turk'.

In this market Edmonia Lewis could not fail.

Carving in marble, or modelling in clay, she provided it as eagerly as any with the busts and sculptured romances it demanded; but the busts mostly portrayed champions of liberty, while the romances came from the Bible or Longfellow—*Hiawatha* offered almost imperative themes for an artist who was as much Amerindian as she was Negro. Her romantic neo-classicism accordingly departed from the Greek ideal—and in the departure some critics saw the projection of an original mind. Henry Tuckerman, the leading historian of American art in the nineteenth century, thought she was 'unquestionably the most interesting representative of our country in Europe. . . .' Perhaps she would infuse the American school with a style which was 'distinctive, if not entirely original'.

But 'the youthful Indian girl in the Via della Frezza', long away from her roots and perhaps frustrated by personal problems, was already petering out when Tuckerman wrote, though the illusion of further creativity remained: she sent many interesting works to the vast Memorial Hall set up to celebrate culture in the labyrinthine vulgarity of the Philadelphia Centennial Exposition of 1876. Dwarfed by tortured marbles of colossal size, her *Death of Cleopatra* was nevertheless praised for its 'striking qualities' and evidence of 'genuine endowments'. She never excelled it.

In fact, Edmonia's brief vogue, in spite of many subsequent commissions, had all but ended. The Greek Revival was dying: an unconscious symbol of its decay was a much admired *Sleeping Iolanthe* in butter at the Exposition. And the great days of the stalwarts were all but over: Charles Sumner (plate 19) was among the last. New days, new ways, new men were there, but she was too far away in space and manner, too fixed in her themes, to encompass them. Near the top, she sank into complete obscurity. Her end, like her beginning, is a mystery or a conspiracy of silence. Even the year of her death is uncertain.

Two more women, Meta Vaux Warrick (Mrs Fuller) and May Howard Jackson, followed Edmonia Lewis. Both were born in Philadelphia in 1877 and both had their art training there. Meta Warrick also studied at the Académie Colarossi in Paris, where Rodin thought her promising. Her style, though largely his, was more employed in the expression of suffering than sensuousness and she became known as a delicate 'sculptor of horrors'. Her community needed one, but when she exhibited in 1914, four years after a fire had destroyed most of her works, emotional depth had given way to simply expressed charm—and she was a very charming person indeed. The difficulty of obtaining good pictures of her works has confined us to illustrating a single example (plate 19).

May Jackson refused the lures of Paris. Never outstanding as a thematic modeller, she excelled at forthright portraits of forthright men. Her bust of Kelly Miller (1863–1939), a leading personality of Howard University, Washington, D.C., is typical (plate 19). It will be better understood if we extract a few sentences from an open letter he wrote in 1905 to Thomas Dixon, a fiery defender of the Old South from whom D. W. Griffiths took the treatment of the first spectacular film, *The Birth of a Nation* (1914):

> You are a white man born in the midst of the civil war, I am a Negro born during the same stirring epoch. You were born with a silver spoon in your mouth, I was born with an iron hoe in my hand. Your race has inflicted accumulated injury and wrong upon mine, mine has borne yours only service and good will. . . . You stir the slumbering fires of race wrath into an uncontrollable flame. . . . You poison the mind and pollute the imagination. . . . But do not think, Mr Dixon, that when you evoke the evil spirit, you can exorcise him at will. The Negro in the end will be the least of his victims. Those who become inoculated with the virus of race hatred are more unfortunate than the victims of it. . . . You are a greater enemy to your own race than you are to mine. . . .

Henry Tanner (1859–1937) brought the journeyman period of American Negro art, in Alain Locke's phrase, to its peak. A weak-looking man, uncritical and egotistic, he had the capacity, as weak men often do, of choosing a career and pursuing it with increasing skill. Disapproval of his choice did not prevent his father, a bishop in the African Methodist Episcopal Church, from supporting him at the Pennsylvania Academy of the Fine Arts. There he took from Thomas Eakins, aptly described by Oliver Larkin as 'an artistic surgeon in an age of quacks', everything that application could take, except the master's fundamental advice (quoted by Larkin):

> If America is to produce great painters and if young art students wish to assume a place in the history of the art of their country, their first desire should be to remain in America, to peer deeper into the heart of American life.

After graduating in 1888, Tanner taught in Atlanta, sold photographs, and painted animals, landscapes and people. His *Banjo Lesson* (plate 23) promised that at last Negro life would inspire a Negro genre painter of exceptional power, but Tanner was already looking across the Atlantic. The help of two bishops of his church provided the funds for escape and in 1891 he was sitting at the feet of Benjamin Constant in the Académie Julian, Paris. His nostalgic tales of those happy years included the usual emphasis on struggle: it amounted to no more than genteel poverty.

At the Académie he applied its lessons to impressions of life in Brittany and Normandy, but he also matured a personal style influenced by the earlier discipline of Eakins, his admiration for Rembrandt, and his studies in Palestine at the expense of Rodman Wanamaker. The Holy Land settled his interest in a form of romantic orientalism which brought him success after the *Resurrection of Lazarus* won a minor medal in the Salon of 1897.

It was scarcely a 'sensation', but it was purchased by the government (who seem to have lost it in the confusions following the Second World War), and it created an interest which soon took Tanner into the leading private and institutional collections in America. Deservedly so, for his Biblical pictures, set in his lavishly equipped studio with the care of a stage director, are intriguingly contrived masterpieces of composition, colour harmony, and the play of light. We reproduce two outstanding examples (plates 22, 24) and, for comparison, an attractive return to genre (plate 22). Unfortunately, space could not be found for his dramatic 'close up' of *Two Disciples at the Tomb* in the Art Institute of Chicago.

American appreciation kept the 'dean of American painters' comfortably aloof in Paris for forty-six years. He liked the rôle of an expatriate phenomenon in search of artistic truth; and coloured artists who sought his help were accordingly reminded that they could have it as artists, not Negroes. So, above nationality and group loyalty, he spent the last twenty years of his life in increasing isolation and decline; for no book, even when it is the Bible, can last an artist for 'ever'. Long forgotten in France, unknown elsewhere in Europe, his name now survives in America by the circumstance of birth and the perpetuating will of historically minded Negroes. The irony should be educative.

With one exception, William Harper (1873–1910), Tanner was the first and last of the significant Negro painters of the nineteenth century and its cultural intrusion into the twentieth. Harper had a technical command and poetic vision, alert to new trends, which should have brought a lively mind and master's palette into the resurgence of American art after the First World War. But his death at twenty-seven left no more than a small collection of delightful sketches and paintings, made mostly in Brittany, Provence, Southern England and Mexico, which have not been seen since the Memorial Exhibition at the Art Institute of Chicago in 1910. It is most regrettable that efforts to represent him in this book have only secured the landscape reproduced (plate 24). It does not show him at his best.

THE NEW NEGRO

Time and an ocean separate the American Negro from his African ancestors. 'What is Africa to me?' cried Countee Cullen in the 'twenties, showing in his Ceylonese 'spicy grove and cinnamon tree' that it was not even 'a book one thumbs'. But the question was being asked and the answers nourished the flowering of the 'Negro Renaissance'.

Understandably, it was a late flowering. The 'twenties opened before the Negro *avant garde* appreciated the cultural developments upon which it could draw. In Paris, Guillaume Apollinaire and his friends had added to *l'art moderne* the fertilizing quality of *l'art nègre*. In New York, the alarming glimpses of new directions offered by Alfred Stieglitz at his Gallery 291 had led to the more cautious,

Palmer Hayden
Fétiche et Fleurs

Harmon
Foundation

The first important still-life of the Negro Renaissance. Fetishes were in the mood

though still frightening, Armory Show of February 1913 in the armoury of the Sixty-ninth Cavalry Regiment at New York. Many of its eleven hundred works, representing every trend in modern art, attracted the attentions of mob-crazy louts, whom Marcel Duchamp's *Nude Descending a Staircase* roused to the screaming frenzy of deprival: there was a staircase, but the titillating nude who should have been descending it looked like the dynamited parts of five bodies in a flowing reassemblage. Today, that staircase is old-fashioned.

Poetry, for obvious reasons, made an earlier and deeper impact. High school boys and girls knew something of the revolutionary accumulation from Walt Whitman to Carl Sandburg; and the 'fat black bucks' of Vachel Lindsay's mumbo-jumbo *Congo* (1914)

had whacked some receptive browns with a terrific 'Boomlay, boomlay, boomlay, BOOM.'

One of these youths, rich in the stirrings of seventeen, was on his way to Texas in the winter of 1919. Beyond St. Louis, as his train rocked from loop to loop of the Mississippi in the picture-making dusk, his thoughts, circling beyond the bounty and wrath of the 'onrestless river' into Time and certainty and ethnic pride, shaped a poem on the back of an old envelope:

I've known rivers:
I've known rivers ancient as the world and older than
   the flow of human blood in human veins.
My soul has grown deep like the rivers.
I bathed in the Euphrates when dawns were young,
I built my hut near the Congo and it lulled me to sleep,
I looked upon the Nile and raised the pyramids above
   it.
I heard the singing of the Mississippi when Abe Lincoln
   went down to New Orleans, and I've seen its muddy
   bosom turn all golden in the sunset.
I've known rivers:
Ancient, dusky rivers.
My soul has grown deep like the rivers.

This poem, more reprinted and recited than any other American poem of the last forty years, was published by W. E. B. Du Bois in *The Crisis* for June 1921—in that year the Afro-French writer, René Maran, won the *Prix Goncourt* with his *Batouala*. *The Negro Speaks of Rivers* ushered in and set the tone of the Negro Renaissance; and its author, Langston Hughes, became the poet of the New Negro. Almost at the same time, the movement found its painter in Aaron Douglas, a young man addicted to the notion that the ultimate purposes of painting, like poetry ('poet' means 'myth-maker'), are to chronicle history, reveal thought and transform myths.

The Renaissance was fortunate, too, in finding its philosopher in a professor of philosophy and roving aesthete, Alain Locke, still lightly yoked to Harvard, Oxford and Berlin. His sophisticated interests—he lived in the market place too—ranged from the problems of values and cultural pluralism, by way of the applications of philosophy to human relations, to all the arts. Locke mirrored and led the movement in a historic number of the *Survey Graphic* (March 1925), elaborated nine months later into a sumptuous book, *The New Negro*. Alfred Knopf missed publishing it, but thereafter, closely rivalled by the Viking Press, he became the principal sponsor of progressive Negro writing.

The timing of *The New Negro* could not have been

better. Immediately behind it were major anthologies of American Negro poetry and spirituals by James Weldon Johnson; books of poems by Claude McKay, *Harlem Shadows*, and Countee Cullen, *Color*; several competent novels; *The Gift of Black Folk* by W. E. B. Du Bois; the founding of *Opportunity*, in which Charles Johnson encouraged creative expression; and the somewhat tropicalized success of Negroes in music and drama. Carl Van Vechten's *Nigger Heaven*, Langston Hughes' *The Weary Blues*, W. C. Handy's *Treasury of the Blues* (illustrated by Miguel Covarrubias), and several more novels, appeared in the following year. Above all, Mr Van Vechten himself became an adopted Negro, with very beneficial results to Negro institutions and creativity.

The only Negro artist presented by *The New Negro* was Aaron Douglas. The geometric symbolism of his illustrations for it moved forward quickly into the illuminated shades and contrasts, integrated with a classical sense of proportion and interval, of his suggestive illustrations for James Weldon Johnson's *God's Trombones: Seven Negro Sermons in Verse* (1927). These transformed folk sermons conveyed the imagery and manner of the fundamentalist Negro minister in highly sophisticated verse; and Douglas pictorialized that imagery in a way that remains unique in book illustration.

Deprived of the opportunity to collaborate again with a creative writer of equal stature, Douglas developed his particular symbolic style in his murals (end papers and plate 26). Criticisms of them in terms of elongation and angularities, patterns of mystical light, implausible exoticism and so on are merely trite. The importance of his murals is that they com-

municate their intentions in an original and satisfying way, without benefit from any school. His expression of light, in Sir Kenneth Clark's phrase, is an 'expression of love'.

Other artists soon followed Aaron Douglas into the Renaissance and some were dragged, temporarily, into it. His own description of what happened is just enough exaggerated to emphasize the truth:

> Harlem was sifted. Neither streets, homes nor public institutions escaped. When unsuspecting Negroes were found with a brush in their hands they were immediately hauled away and held for interpretation. They were given places of honour and bowed to with much ceremony. Every effort to protest their innocence was drowned out with big-mouthed praise. A number escaped and returned to a more reasonable existence. Many fell in with the game and went along making hollow and meaningless gestures with brush and palette.
> But . . . the Negro artists have emerged . . .

Their emergence was celebrated in January 1928 by the Harmon Foundation at International House, New York, in the first all-Negro exhibition in America. Some of the eighty-seven items were oddments of schoolgirl standard, but the majority were more than creditable. Apart from Aaron Douglas, many of the exhibitors became, and remained, eminent in American Negro art: Augusta Savage and Sargent Johnson among the sculptors, Allan Freelon, John Hardrick, Palmer Hayden, Malvin Gray Johnson, James Porter, William Scott, Laura Wheeler Waring and Hale Woodruff among the painters. The photographic work involved was done by James Latimer Allen, the pioneer Negro creative photographer.

Archibald Motley, winner of the Harmon Gold Award for 1928, was not included as his pictures were being shown at the New Galleries. May Howard Jackson received the Bronze Award, though her work was also not available. William Johnson won the Gold Award in 1929, though he did not exhibit until 1930; and Nancy Elizabeth Prophet took a prize, though she too did not exhibit until 1930. Motley and Richmond Barthé joined the Harmon exhibit in 1929; Allan Crite, Lois Jones and Ellis Wilson in 1930; William Cooper, Meta Fuller, James Wells (winner of the Gold Award in 1930), Edwin Harleston and May Howard Jackson in 1931.

By 1933, William Artis, Henry Bannarn, Leslie Bolling, Joseph Carter, Samuel Brown, Beauford DeLaney, Elton Fax and Romeyn Van Vleck Lippman were among the hundred and twenty-five artists who had taken advantage of the facilities offered by the Foundation. These included five exhibitions, travelling exhibits seen by nearly half a million

Aaron Douglas
Alexandre Dumas
In support of his Negritude the Negro looked attentively abroad

31

people in fifty cities, co-operation in several exhibitions, the promotion of art education in Negro schools and colleges, and much other assistance. A new situation, marked by the Whitney Museum's purchase of Nancy Prophet's *Congolaise* and three works by Barthé, had been created.

Critics of the Harmon Foundation's activities failed to realize that, while patronizing mediocrity, it was also sponsoring the makers of modern Negro art; and that one of its most important services was the provision of opportunities for critics to criticize. Romare Bearden, then a student, was severe:

> Many of the Negro artists argue that . . . since the Negro is becoming so amalgamated with the white race, and has accepted the white man's civilization he must progress along those lines. Even if this is true, they are certainly not taking advantage of the Negro scene. The Negro in his various environments in America, holds a great variety of rich experiences for the genuine artists. . . . Instead, the Negro artist will proudly exhibit his 'Scandinavian Landscape', a locale that is entirely alien to him. This will of course impress the uninitiated who, through some feeling of inferiority toward their own subject matter, only require that a work of art have some sort of foreign stamp to make it acceptable. . . .

> No one can doubt that the Negro is possessed of remarkable gifts of imagination and intuition. When he has learned to harness his great gifts of rhythm and pours it into his art—his chance of creating something individual will be heightened. At present it seems that by a slow study of rules and formulas the Negro artist is attempting to do something with his intellect, which he has not felt emotionally. In consequence he has given us poor echoes of the work of white artists—and nothing of himself. . . .

> There are quite a few foundations that sponsor exhibitions of the work of Negro artists. . . . Take for instance the Harmon Foundation. . . . It has encouraged the artist to exhibit long before he has mastered the technical equipment of his medium. By its choice of the type of work it favors, it has allowed the Negro artist to accept standards that are both artificial and corrupt. . . .

> The artist must be the medium through which humanity expresses itself. In this sense the greatest artists have faced the realities of life, and have been profoundly social. . . . An intense, eager devotion to present day life, to study it, to help relieve it, this is the calling of the Negro artist.

The fundamental truths in Mr Bearden's assessment remain true. What it overlooked was that the making of good art amongst underprivileged peoples is necessarily accompanied by the making of much more bad art; that it would be unwise for an encouraging organization to pontificate on what is good and bad, especially as time changes viewpoints and matures some artists at least; and that most of the artists for whom the Harmon Foundation opened doors were doing just what Mr Bearden required. They were facing realities; they were relieving the burdens of living; they were chronicling, interpreting and sometimes transforming. In doing so, they were meeting the needs of their own people—and the ultimate test of any work of art is its value to the society in which it is produced, not its reception by the coteries as amusing, exotic, exciting, interesting, original or universal.

Universal art does not arise from the intention to be universal: it is sifted out of deeply rooted community art. 'The artist must work in contact with society,' Henry Moore told a Unesco conference a few years ago, 'but that contact must be an intimate one. I believe that the best artists have always had their roots in a definite social group or community, or in a particular region. We know what small and intimate communities produced the great sculpture of Athens, or Chartres, or Florence.'

The Negro artist is fortunate in belonging to a definite group organized as regional communities; and within the group is a pulsing folkart, and pervading urgencies of mythology, conditions, circumstances and viewpoints, for absorption, transformation and return to the group as works of art. The Negro Renaissance began the work of drawing upon the inspirations of this living classicism, but was inevitably motivated much more by 'race' pride. The fact that there are no races, that all human groups are mongrelized, has seldom disturbed such satisfactions.

Richmond Barthé
Langston Hughes (1930)
The Poet of the New Negro

32

The rediscovery of African culture, and 'the legacy of the ancestral arts', therefore offered hopes of racial inheritance, but actually produced little more in poetry than desires to see 'slim palm trees pulling at the clouds' or other arboreal phenomena. The visual arts accordingly gained colour, but Alain Locke was compelled to admit in 1940 that 'when the younger Negro artists first became aware of this heritage, a sudden and hectic interest flared up which led, unfortunately, to relatively superficial under-standing and shallow artistic results. African art could yield little through direct imitation or sophis-ticated racial pride.'

Nevertheless, he thought that African art could 'still have rich inspiration to offer to any artist, but especially to a group of artists who may sense or cultivate a close spiritual kinship with it'. It may be that he was more prophetic than his critics knew, for there are indications that the upsurge of African nationalisms will give American Negroes greatly increased opportunities for extending their cultural understanding and contributing to African needs. The activities of the American Society of African Culture, New York, and the superb special number of *Présence Africaine* edited by the Executive Director of the Society, John A. Davis, promise a happy future for co-operation between Africans, West Indians and American Negroes. One hopes it will not be afflicted, as Indian friendships were by J. Saunders Redding (*An American in India*), by ex-radicals turned near-pukka sahibs.

It should be recognized, too, that sentimental Africanism prompted new values basic to group pride. Concepts of feminine beauty in Negro litera-ture, so important in this respect, moved con-spicuously in the direction of the variously expressed preferences of the common people: 'a sealskin brown make the preacher lay his Bible down'; 'the blacker the berry, the sweeter the juice'. A study, for example, by Cynthia Mathis (in the thesis Library of Fisk University) of seventy-one novels by Negroes from 1886 to 1936 showed an increasing preference for dark skins, especially after 1920: of 147 beautiful women among their characters, twenty-five were white, fifty-six yellow, fifty-six brown and ten black, the whites being in the earlier, and the blacks in the later, works.

The Negro poets of the 'twenties rejected the octoroon sirens of Lafcadio Hearn. Dancing round the fires of supposedly racial bacchanals, they chanted the praises of the Golden Brown. 'That brown girl's swagger gives a twitch to beauty like a queen', sang Countee Cullen, whose poetic philo-sophy, excluding love from intimacy with the 'milk-white maiden', affirmed that 'Who lies with his nut-

James Porter *Courtesy*
In an early sketchbook *Robert Scurlock*
Nude studies by Negro artists were rare before 1925

brown maiden. . . . He lies, and his love lies there.'

Frank Horne, himself as light as any dark man could wish, declared that 'A brown woman's beauty can make you feel good all over'; and Langston Hughes went to the jungle to suggest the reason why: 'What jungle tree have you slept under, night-dark girl of the swaying hips?' The notion lingers, very attractively, in Rex Goreleigh's *Jungle Dancer* (plate 95).

The girls sang brownfully, too, though in rather sweet soprano voices. The deep contralto of young Helene Johnson, the most forthright hedonist of the Renaissance, was a striking exception. She went straight to the point: 'Gee, brown boy, I loves you all over. I'm glad I'm a jig. I'm glad I can under-stand your dancin' and your singin' and feel all the happiness and joy and don't-care in you.'

Interestingly, no images of black beauty were created: even Claude McKay, the most black-conscious of the New Negro writers, preferred 'dark', 'swarthy', and 'bronze' in his poems. Edward Silvera did, however, remark that:

There is beauty
In the faces of black women,
Jungle beauty
And mystery
Dark hidden beauty
In the faces of black women,
Which only black men
See.

The cult of dark paganism naturally required conditions in which the jig-wa, and its mutabilities, could flourish. Indeed, more than places to make love in, the ultimate fullness of love depends on a feeling of possessing and being possessed by all that lies around and beyond them; and the quickening of this feeling, with struggle as its extension and no hope

33

of early fulfilment, has always been a major task for poetry and the arts. Its importance in the Negro situation matches the dimensions of privations that arise from the other extreme of the national misfortune put in six inspired lines by Robert Frost:

The land was ours before we were the land's.
She was our land more than a hundred years
Before we were her people. She was ours . . .
But we were still England's, still colonials,
Possessing what we still were unpossessed by,
Possessed by what we now no more possessed.

James Weldon Johnson was one of the earlier poets who knew that the possessing land must be possessed, but his poems contain little more than the certainty of victory for the 'upward, onward, marching host', who had 'bought a rightful sonship here' (*Fifty Years*, 1913). In the 'twenties, Langston Hughes concluded *The Weary Blues* with the companionable assurance that 'Tomorrow, I'll sit at the table when company comes', for 'I, too, am America'; and before him Claude McKay confessed that he loved 'this cultured hell that tests my youth!' And loving it, he looked 'into the days ahead' and saw its 'might and granite wonders there, beneath the touch of Time's unerring hand, like priceless treasures sinking in the sand'.

Twenty years passed before these supplements to Edgar Lee Masters' vision 'of a New Republic, brighter than the sun' were transformed by Margaret Walker into images of living and loving within the tension of deprival:

I want my body bathed again by southern suns . . .
I want to rest again in southern fields, in grass and hay and clover bloom . . .
I want my rest unbroken in the fields of southern earth; freedom to watch the corn wave silver in the sun and mark the splashing of a brook . . .
I want my careless song to strike no minor key; no fiend to stand between my body's southern song—the fusion of the South, my body's song and me.

On a more immediate scale, sentiments of identification were frequently expressed by the New Negro poets. They brought to Negro literature and the arts a fresh awareness that a man's home is his own, even when he cannot pay the rent. It is his personal reality, surrounded by sights and sounds and smells that are the life-stuff on which he grows. His river may be full of alligators and its banks reminiscent of horror, his woods peopled by the shrieking ghosts of burning men, his avenues trodden by generations who sat on the kerbstones grieving their hearts and souls—but they are his own.

Previously, Paul Laurence Dunbar had made the cabin in the cotton (Pippin, plate 10), with mammy

Robert Blackburn
Upper New York
The possessing land must be possessed

*Courtesy Barnett
Aden Gallery*

saying the blessing over the corn pone and chitterlings, seem like the heaven it never was; and James Weldon Johnson had immortalized Manhattan in *My City*; but now it was Harlem, the city within a city, that touched the Negro lyre. Its music was a discovery communicated by Langston Hughes, the poet, above all, of Harlem:

Strange,
That in this nigger place
I should meet life face to face;
When, for years, I had been seeking
Life in places gentler-speaking,
Until I came to this vile street
And found Life stepping on my feet!

Thereafter, Negro poetry throbbed with the impact of Harlem, Memphis, Atlanta and other cities where life teemed in the streets; of the golden cornlands of Sterling Brown, where unattainable women were as 'purty as Kingdom Come' and 'de red licker's good'; and of black folk, some climbing and some defeated by the next step, some beautiful and some lovely beyond beauty, for whom Life, in Langston Hughes' unforgettable phrase, 'ain't been no crystal stair'.

And, as artists are poets too, they soon joined this ferment of awareness. Some came out of the studios of yesterday to add inspired documentation of people and places; others interpreted the spirit of their time. A glimpse of their achievements is afforded by several pictures in the text and plates of this book.

Aaron Douglas found no rival in the symbolic treatment of themes, but in realistic portraiture (plate facing p. 32; pp. 11, 31, 47) he acknowledged an equal in Archibald Motley (plates 33, 34): epochs lived in Mr Motley's portraits. James Porter, then barely past the young student stage, was moving into the company of these older men as an interpreter of the Negro face. His drawings had the swift gripping precision of a Delacroix; his oils were revelations of the soul. Unfortunately destroyed by fire, his very early *Sarah* (1928) remains in reproduction (plate 36) one of the most haunting portraits in Negro art. The same quality of brooding beyond personal distress lives in his *Woman Holding a Jug*, but it gives more than a hint of previously resisted indulgence in the decorative temptations to which his mature style succumbed. His attractive tribute to Dorothy Porter (plate 36), a leading figure in the world of Negro scholarship, is an example.

Neither Douglas nor Porter painted a period. Motley did. In fact, no other Negro artist reflected the preoccupations of the 'twenties and their aftermath more typically and interestingly: a Roman Catholic born in New Orleans, with a proud claim to part-Pygmy ancestry, he was emotionally fitted to do so. He gave a decade tortured by racial mystiques the exquisite torture of superb pictures of the *fille de couleur* which brought Lafcadio Hearn's ecstasies to the eye, for each one was a 'thoroughbred representing the true secret of grace—economy of force'.

He also left us a series of evocative impressions of Negro and Parisian night life which belong to the history of an age. They are social comments but not satires. The compassion of true artistry, the communicated flow of rhythm and misdirected vitality, raise them above caricature. We reproduce four (plates 52, 62).

Mr Motley was alone, too, in taking Africanism seriously. He did not look to it for motifs or lessons in design; he did the artist's job of trying to transform various tribal myths in his own manner. His 'symbolic realism' visualized the control of nature by magic, but the dark continent was still so dark and full of Voodoo that critics saw in his African pictures no more than the exuberant treatment of rank vegetation, lurking terror, the mystery of tropical moons, and savage submission to sorcery. Edward Alden Jewell stood before them bewitched:

> Vivid pictures they are and weirdly unique their subjects. Here are steaming jungles that drip and sigh and ooze, dank in the impenetrable gloom of palm and woven tropical verdure, or ablaze with light where the sun breaks fiercely in. Here are moons that rise, yellow and round, quizzical and portentous, aureoled with a pallor of sorcery; crescent moons with secrets cryptically packed in the shining scimitar, and moons that wane and die with a shudder of spent prophecy. . . . There are devil-devils watching in the solemn night or poised to swoop on hapless human prey. There are

James Porter
An Early Drawing
The swift precision of a Delacroix

thunders and lightnings with revelation imprisoned in their heart of death. There are charms, simple or unsearchable, to lure a smile or to ravage with the hate of vampires!

> Glistening dusky bodies, stamping or gliding, shouting or silent, are silhouetted against hot ritual fires. Myriad age-old racial memories drift up from Africa and glowing islands of the sea. . . .

It is truly a period piece, magnificently meaningless, for an anthologist of the 'twenties. Nothing is said about the intention of the pictures, but Mr Jewell did determine a considerable effort to reproduce at least one in this book. Unfortunately, it did not succeed.

Among the sculptors of the 'twenties, though Meta Fuller and May Jackson reached new heights and Richmond Barthé looked promising, the only evidence of a definitely new talent was seen in the exquisite spare-time works, contemporary in feeling and entirely uncluttered by virtuosity, of Sargent Johnson. His versatility extended to porcelain, terra cotta, bronze and wood, and sometimes he achieved unusual effects in combined media (such as porcelain and bronze), but he is best known for his ceramic polychrome sculpture. Regrettably, space prevents more than a glimpse (plates 73, 74) of the many achievements of this refreshingly outstanding artist whose maturity shows no less of *élan*.

35

PROGRESS AND PROBLEMS

Before the First World War one of the many lily-white novels, Robert Lee Durham's *The Call of the South*, that tore at good hearts in the dear old Southland told the terrible story of a president's daughter who accepted as white a talented, heroic Harvard man in whom the black drop lurked. One night the couple took refuge from a storm in a wayside hut; and then, of course, it happened:

> Helen is quiescent in his arms for a short space and suffers his caresses. Suddenly startled, she looks at his face—distorted! With a shriek of terror she wildly tries to push him from her; but the demon of the blood of Guinea Gumbo is pitiless, and against the fury of it, as against the storm, she fights and cries—in vain.

In the 'twenties the blood of Guinea Gumbo remained irresistibly pitiless in the new dimensions of pseudo-science. Lothrop Stoddard and others aggravated fear of *The Rising Tide of Colour* into a Eur-American neurosis; and the 'newer genetical anthropology', which was older than Gobineau and Houston Stewart Chamberlain, confirmed the immutability of race and the distressing consequences of mongrelizing mongrels. Negro scholars, on the whole, did not contest this massive nonsense. They took the easier course of investing The Race, an absurd phrase still common in all kinds of Negro writing, with qualities as good as, and better than, that of any other non-existent race.

The result has been a monumental confusion, not least amongst Negro creative workers. Artists addicted to the concept of race bravely deny 'racial qualities' in American Negro art. Their art, like themselves, is American or 'universal'. Their opponents thump the race drum with studied exuberance: for them The Race has 'racial memories' and a peculiar heritage awaiting racial expression.

Yet the truth is simple. The Negroes of the United States form an organized minority group within the nation. Thus, they are Negroes as well as Americans; and their art as a whole must reflect their minority condition as well as the larger influences around them. It is both Negro and American because those who make it are Negroes, in the American sense, and Americans. In short, American Negro art is a fully American art.

Some Negro artists will, therefore, lean heavily towards being Americans; and illusions of integration, enlarged by personal acceptance within their particular circles, will encourage them to bend over till they fall down. Others will respond more to their 'Negritude' than to Americanism, but a strong sense

of sympathy and affinity, prompting a fresh search for values and ideas in Africa or elsewhere, can become dangerous if it develops into racialism. At the same time, the quality of affirmation in Africanism should make it more productive than Negro Americanism, in which the sterilizing element of denial is often pathetically evident.

The Negro Renaissance illustrates this brief analysis. Underlying its Africanism was the intention to retaliate against racialism in racial terms. The Race was a phenomenon of group pride, without living roots in Africa (though there were cultural survivals in America) or justification in biology, which could not contain the 'ancestral legacies' offered it by Alain Locke and his supporters. Nevertheless, because it was an affirmation, the Africanism of the Renaissance produced interesting experiments and widened horizons in American Negro culture. Indeed, even the statement of sophisticated Africanism was not possible without participation in the prevailing cultural ferment. A new way of looking, sensitized by the association of blackness with heritage, at the Negroness of Negroes at home was accordingly developed which freshened the quality, and multiplied the quantity, of artistic documentation and interpretation.

Certainly, there was more to look at than ever before. The citywards movement which began after the Emancipation still left four-fifths of the Negro population in the rural South in 1890, while Southern towns accommodated about seven-tenths of the urban Negroes in 1910. During the next twenty years the movements of some 2 million Negroes were largely to the North, where the Negro population increased from 1,027,674 in 1910 to 2,409,219 in 1930. Philadelphia, Chicago, Detroit and New York, where two-fifths of the Northern Negroes now live, were the favoured cities. Chicago, a major cultural centre, had 109,458 Negroes in 1920 against 44,103 in 1910. Harlem, a white residential area of New York in 1900 which a few Negro families had penetrated by 1906, became the 'black metropolis' of the world by 1920.

This internal migration, the most spectacular in history, brought the personalities, lives, loves, heroes, troubles and successes of Negroes to artistic attention, both white and coloured, in ways and urgencies previously unknown. There could have been no Negro Renaissance without it—a Renaissance so completely unique in American history, even if we compare it with the cultural expansion in the days of Philip Freneau, that it deserves the name.

The force of this upsurge is not yet spent, though

some Negroes, overwhelmed by the notion that it was an explosion of the gay 'twenties, allow the Depression to submerge it. Actually, it moved towards its peak in the 'thirties and early 'forties, for the influencing circumstances intensified and widened, Negro writers and artists matured, their audiences increased, some Negro schools and colleges became more alert to their responsibilities, philanthropic funds were available to creative workers, and all found greater security and stimulation in the culture-making Roosevelt Era than they had known before.

Many Negro artists now had the advantage of study in such great art centres as Philadelphia, Chicago and New York, with the additional *cachet* of experience in Europe, where the Académie Julian and the Académie Colarossi had become the ateliers favoured by tradition. These pioneers realized that the paths they had followed were for the few. The growth of artistic productivity and appreciation by

Negroes depended, they knew, on an enveloping climate of art in Negro homes, schools, colleges and communities. At the same time many Negro educators acquired the not strictly comparable notion that the facilities of a liberal college should include an art department, providing it did not encourage sin or otherwise get too liberal.

Old art departments were accordingly expanded and new ones created. At Howard University, Washington, D.C., James Herring was fortunate in being joined by James Porter, Lois Mailou Jones, James Lesesne Wells and Alonzo Aden; and time has shown that they were perhaps wiser than they knew in accepting the hovering presence of Alain Locke as an irritant to be more or less stoically borne.

Fisk University, Nashville, Tennessee, secured in Aaron Douglas a teacher who believed in 'the hard way', along which, as a campus editor once complained, he occasionally distributed 'praise in weak

James Wells
East River

Better conditions brought some two million Negroes to the North between 1910 and 1920

Courtesy International Business Machines Corp.

microscopic pills'. Those, like Gregory Ridley (plate 72), who survived the professor's inability to mollycoddle became artists.

Atlanta University found in Hale Woodruff a brilliant and zestful teacher and Woodruff found there the opportunity to express in forceful ways the clamouring abundance of subjects and themes that surrounded him. His inspiring example, charming personality, and gift for demonstrating techniques and ideas soon inflamed a group which enjoyed as a compliment the designation 'Outhouse School'. Fred Flemister (plates 38, 51) and Wilmer Jennings (page 111) were among its most outstanding members.

In recent years, flourishing art departments have grown in many Negro colleges. Those built around John Biggers at Texas Southern University (Houston), James Parks at Lincoln University (Jefferson City, Missouri), Hayward Oubré at Alabama State College (Montgomery, Alabama), Ed Wilson at North Carolina College (Durham, N.C.), Harper Phillips at Grambling College (Grambling, Louisiana), Phillip Hampton at Savannah State College (Savannah, Georgia), John Howard at Arkansas A.M. and N. College (Pine Bluff, Arkansas), David Driskell at Talladega College (Talladega, Alabama), Ophelia Andrews at West Virginia State College (Institute, W. Virginia), and James Lewis at Morgan State College (Baltimore) are among many more that would raise this list to a directory.

With co-operative redistribution of their properties, and help from the foundations, these institutions could establish regional museums in which every American Negro artist of consequence would be represented, keeping for themselves teaching collections introducing world art, the art of the Americas, and American Negro art, with emphasis on local successes. Meanwhile, Howard University takes pride in owning over 1,000 works of art, while Fisk University boasts, on suitable occasions, of its considerable Alfred Stieglitz Collection donated by Georgia O'Keefe 'with the hope that it may show that there are many ways of seeing and thinking, and possibly, . . . give some one confidence in his own way . . .' More than a decade has passed without news that anyone at Fisk has found confidence through this endearingly quixotic gift, but

James Wells
Shipyard 1948

American Negro workers have a long history of experience in industrial production

Hale Woodruff   Cedric Dover
Sunday Promenade 1939
The Atlanta School, especially known for its printmakers, grew
round the inspiring teaching of Mr Woodruff

degrees. Overloaded teachers, respectably certificated, have little opportunity to build schools around their personalities and achievements. Instead, they cope with a multitude of duties, tend to find comfort in their versatility, and are required to produce departmental successes partly by publicizing talented students who should be advised to put their class exercises away as souvenirs. Critical standards are accordingly obscured, personal conceits fostered, and community achievements disproportionately stressed, by a flow of words and illustrations which, as Elizabeth Catlett says, 'have accomplished little more than the preservation of a great mass of mediocre work and potential talent as representative of artistic accomplishment among Negroes'.

Consequently, until quite recently, the art workshops and community art centres, which multiplied during the 'thirties through local enthusiasm and government aid, generally produced more art than the colleges. In Harlem, the interrelated activities of the Artists Guild, the Art Centre, the Art Workshop, the Alston-Bannarn Studios and the Public Library, with the advantage of a flow of talent to and from

there is no doubt that its expansion and reorganization would be definitely beneficial.

The recent appointment of Samuel Green to the art department of Tuskegee Institute (Tuskegee, Alabama) might, if Mr Green's courage matches his exceptionally high qualifications as an art curator, edge its Museum of Negro Art and Culture out of the world of Booker T. Washington in which it slumbers. Repeated efforts to represent it in this book eventually resulted in four photographs, including a revealing picture of Mr Washington and his sons on their morning ride, publicizing the founder. This appreciated courtesy gained emphasis from the inability of several tired presidents of Negro colleges to acknowledge letters.

In such experiences there is a hint that academic progress in American Negro art still finds 'little co-operation from the administration in exploring the full possibilities of an art programme', as Elizabeth Catlett complained in 1944; but artists cannot altogether escape responsibility for administrative attitudes. Wherever the blame lies, the teaching of art in Negro institutions remains confined by a liberal arts syllabus and a phenomenal reliance on

Wilmer Jennings   *Courtesy*
Dead Tree   *Atlanta Univ.*

39

the famous Art Students League, attracted teachers and students of exceptional quality. In Chicago, where the South Side Community Centre was almost an unofficial auxiliary of the renowned Art Institute, Negro art was equally robust; and in Cleveland Negro artists were specially fortunate in the support and facilities given by Karamu House. Several other cities provided comparable facilities.

The workshop approach remains fruitful. John Biggers employs it very successfully, for example, at Texas Southern University; and various private schools run by unusually gifted Negro teachers also function in the best workshop tradition. Among them Allan Freelon continues the life-time of distinguished service to his state at his friendly Windy Crest Studio, Telford, Pennsylvania; and Rex Goreleigh, lately Director of Princeton Group Arts, whose challenging teaching and perpetual pipes are still remembered in Harlem and North Carolina, now surrounds students at his own Studio-on-the-Canal, Princeton, New Jersey, with an atmosphere of hard-working gaiety and, one supposes, tobacco smoke. Serious painters have the further advantage there of working with Hughie Lee-Smith.

The expansion of American creativity in the 'thirties had its economic roots in the projects of the Works Progress Administration under the sympathetic and forward-looking direction of Harry Hopkins —no country in the world was culturally better served by its government in that decade. Free from want and the equally crushing millstone of financial success, and vitalized by the satisfactions of working together for the common good without losing their individuality, the artists sponsored by the W.P.A. established an internationally significant American art. An amply illustrated book on its extent and achievements would be a major contribution to the appreciation of art—and of America.

Negro artists, with the impetus of their own Renaissance to help them, were fully engaged in the national cultural effort. They gave it some of its particular character and they gained for themselves, and their people, a continental extension of experience, opportunity and audience. Aaron Douglas led the way into a new field of Negro art with his wall-decorations in Nashville (Fisk University), Harlem, Chicago and elsewhere; and he was soon followed by Charles Alston, Richmond Barthé, Sargent Johnson, Archibald Motley, Hale Woodruff and others. Their company gained further distinction by the addition of Charles White and Elmer Brown in the early 'forties and of John Biggers, Phillip Hampton, James Parks and Charles Stallings in recent years.

A few of the more important murals by Negro

June Hector
Wild Flowers
An example of recent work in a Negro University

Courtesy Atlanta Univ.

artists are shown in the end papers and plates 25–32. All are, of course, late afterthoughts in architectural decoration, but a project by Carrol Simms, Joseph Mack and John Biggers, for the Science Building of Texas Southern University, on the integration of the theme 'Man and the World of Science' in painting, sculpture and architecture, marks the beginning of a new approach. These artists recognize, in stressing that their designs are limited by a previous architectural plan, that major developments in building will follow close cooperation between architects, artists and prospective users.

The return of Negroes to their early importance in American architecture should be a national asset, for they can bring to it, as Harry Belafonte has said of Charles White's pictures, 'the poetic beauty of Negro idiom'. The effects of that idiom will almost certainly become transforming in thematic exterior decoration when the convention of confining painters to interior murals is discarded; for modern architecture and technology offer fascinating prospects, already indicated by the Library in University City, Mexico, for the artistic treatment of exterior flat surfaces.

The extension of audience, arising from the cultural ferment activated by the W.P.A., also became an increasing gain for American Negro art. The occasional 'one-man shows' of the late 'twenties became relatively frequent events in the leading galleries by 1940; and the collective exhibits of the Harmon Foundation simplified the presentation of art in The Hall of Negro Life, more brusquely called the Federal Negro Building in the official plan, at the Texas Centennial Exposition, Dallas, 1936.

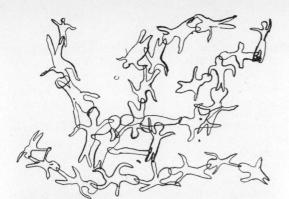
James Dilworth (age 11)

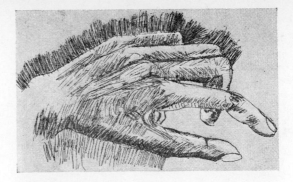
Samuel Dyson (age 12)

'Subnormal' boy (age 11)
Dancers on the stage

'Subnormal boy' (age 11)
Children dancin' in the room, angels dancin' in the sky

CHILDREN'S ART

A critical book on Negro children's art should be of world interest. It should also illuminate many common arguments. For example, there is a definite Negroness about the art of older Negro children, but it comes from surroundings not 'race'. Perhaps there is, too, as we see in the linocuts (the first these boys made), that quality of movement and design which Harry Belafonte sums up as the 'Negro idiom'. The drawings pose questions of education. James Dilworth seems to have retained the imaginativeness of early childhood—or has he transformed a random grouping of the pieces of a jigsaw puzzle? Samuel Dyson, on the other hand, has succumbed to training. Will he become a creative artist who is a masterly draughtsman? Or will he join the parade of imitative talents that come, with much praise, and go forgotten, in each decade?

Top *Courtesy Earl Hooks*
Below *Courtesy Natalie Robinson Cole, author of* The Arts in the Classroom (Day, 1940)

41

Two years later, the New York World Fair gave prominence to *Lift Every Voice* (plate 72), a sculptured group by a dedicated artist, Augusta Savage, whose sensitive skill lives in the work of William Artis (plate 76) and other beneficiaries of her teaching in Harlem. Miss Savage's commission was to convey the spirit of American Negro music, but the theme acquired, 'somehow', a larger purpose emphasized by the reference to James Weldon Johnson's 'Negro National Anthem', which every Negro knows:

Lift every voice and sing
Till earth and heaven ring
Ring with the harmonies of Liberty;
Let our rejoicing rise
High as the listening skies, . . .
Facing the rising sun of our new day begun,
Let us march on till victory is won.

The World Fair was an uneasy jubilation. The Depression was ending, but Europe was nearing another holocaust to save democracy, Asia was astir with intentions to 'throw off the yoke', and the honorary Aryans of Japan were completing arrangements to replace it with a halter gaily inscribed 'Asia for the Asians'. American Negroes read the writing on the wall closely but variously. Some saw in Japan the prospective leader of the coloured world, many supported Indian aspirations vigorously, and the majority knew that proper patriotism must be qualified by increased demands for equal rights. The prevailing attitude was later compressed into the famous 'Double V' slogan of the virile *Pittsburgh Courier:* Victory at home and victory abroad.

How much all this affected the influencing climate of American Negro art during the war years might some day be analysed by a social historian of the quality of Rayford Logan or John Hope Franklin. Meanwhile, it is clear that the remarkable germination of interest in Negro achievements between 1940 and 1945 was accelerated by the domestic situation and the importance of creating good impressions abroad.

Robert Carlen, who belongs in the company of those great dealers who discover and sponsor significant artists, began the period in January 1940 with the Horace Pippin Exhibition at his Galleries in Philadelphia. Albert Barnes of the Barnes Foundation, a good friend of Negro art who had helped to promote the Negro Renaissance, introduced it with a characteristic eulogy which mounted up to the opinion that 'It is probably not too much to say that he (Pippin) is the first important Negro painter to appear on the American scene'. Comparable benedictions quickly established Pippin as a national

figure, whose importance in public relations was so highly appreciated in Washington that he received the Purple Heart in 1945—twenty-seven years after he had been badly wounded in the right arm in France.

An event of greater consequence to American art was the Exhibition of the Art of the American Negro (1851–1940), assembled by Alonzo Aden, with particular co-operation from the Harmon Foundation and the W.P.A., at the American Negro Exposition held at Chicago in the summer of 1940. All the established Negro artists were represented and so were the promising young painters and sculptors who raised the peak of the W.P.A. period—among them William Artis, Robert Blackburn, Selma Burke, Elizabeth Catlett, William Carter, Eldzier Cortor, Fred Flemister, William Jennings, Lois Mailou Jones, Jacob Lawrence, Edward Loper, Hughie-Lee Smith, Charles White and Ellis Wilson soon found the wide recognition they deserved.

Fortunately, the Exhibition also forced Alonzo Aden out of the anonymity of administration into public attention as a young man with a decided flair and a compulsive inclination to help people to enjoy art. Unable to hide himself much longer in the Art Gallery of Howard University, he opened (1943) the Barnett Aden Gallery in his mother's old-fashioned Washington house. There, with James Herring, Alma Thomas and other friends, Mr Aden has consistently fulfilled his intention 'to discover and present new talent, white and coloured, American and foreign, to the community' in the gracious warmth of a charming home. Many of those 'new talents' have now reached international stature, but the Gallery has always offered its visitors more than the excitements of discovery. It is, in fact, a centre of good human relations where pleasures are shared in a lively atmosphere of friendship.

Three months after it closed, the Negro art exhibition at Chicago was perpetuated in expanded form in Alain Locke's classic volume on *The Negro in Art*; and in 1941 people concerned with art in America could scarcely avoid realizing that Negroes were increasing it importantly. McMillen Incorporated, a leading firm of decorators in New York, added to this appreciation a considerable exhibition of Negro art in October; and in December Edith Halpert, a friend of Mary Beattie Brady of the Harmon Foundation, put on an extensive show of *American Negro Art: Nineteenth and Twentieth Centuries* at the Downtown Gallery. It opened two days after the attack on Pearl Harbour.

Jacob Lawrence was the star of Mrs Halpert's successful enterprise. Soon afterwards she hung the

William Artis
A Studio Exhibition
One-man shows by Negro artists are now common throughout the United States

sixty gouache panels of his series on *The Migration of the Negro* and sold them immediately to Mrs David M. Levy, who gave the even numbers to the Museum of Modern Art and the odd numbers to the Phillips Memorial Gallery, it being understood that each institution would show the complete set alternately. This success, following an impressive colour feature in *Fortune* magazine arranged by Miss Brady, allowed a large public to decide whether Lawrence or Pippin was the more outstanding Negro painter. Selden Rodman remained unimpressed. Pippin was his genius, Lawrence a protest painter who 'has never been able to free his style altogether from the suggestion of caricature'. But by 1957 Lawrence had become Mr Rodman's exceptionally exceptional Negro. The citation reads: 'It is generally agreed that he is the ablest painter the Negro race has so far produced in America—perhaps anywhere.'

The war situation prolonged the Downtown Exhibition beyond its closing in New York and eventually evolved it into a national survey (1945), organized by John Davis Hatch for the Albany Institute of History and Art, entitled *The Negro Artist Comes of Age*. According to Mr Hatch, the State Department suggested to Mr Watson of the International Business Machines Corporation that he should buy the whole exhibit for a foreign tour, but what happened is not clear. It circulated in America for some years, apart from a group of thirty-two paintings, prints and sculptures by Negro artists, purchased by the Fine Arts Department of the I.B.M. late in 1947, which have been included in a widely travelled exhibition since then.

The coming of age of the Negro artist was preceded (1943) by James Porter's *Modern Negro Art*, which showed, as Alain Locke and others had done, that the Negro artist was then a sprightly youngster of at least eight score years. Packed with tantalizing clues and tempting arguments, Mr Porter's book is more than an indispensable history. It is a challenge to exploration.

The publication of *Modern Negro Art* coincided more or less with the Second Annual Exhibition of Works by Negro Artists at Atlanta University, where Hale Woodruff knew that the work of his school could stand comparison with the best that Negro artists could produce. Mr Woodruff left Atlanta in 1946, but the Annual Exhibition has continued, with the personal interest of the art-minded President of the University, Rufus Clements, and the brisk fostering of Helen Coulborn, to fulfil a definite need.

Alain Locke hoped, in a foreword to the first catalogue, that the Atlanta exhibitions would 'encourage a healthy and representative art of the people' and promote the 'vitally important task of bringing the Negro artist and his art back to the Southland'; and both these functions were revived in 1959 through co-operation with the National Conference of Negro Artists. This new organization, from which many vigorous local activities have branched, derives its strength from a membership alert to the creative process as a complex artist-audience interaction. Charles White spoke to a united gathering when he hoped that the first Conference would 'serve to inspire our artists to create works permeated with great ideas and great passions' and that it would also 'inspire the Negro people to embrace our works with all their love'. The future of American Negro art is assured by this approach.

43

Alvin Hollingsworth
City Images

Photograph: *Mike Herniter*
Courtesy the Artist

THE CONTINUITY OF NEGRO ART

A society is a grouping of people; its culture is their way of life. The art of a people accordingly begins when they start thinking of themselves as a social group.

The long story of American Negro art proves that this universally observed truth is no less valid in America than it is elsewhere. 'The Negro artist' did not reach his twenty-first birthday in 1945, nor did 'Negroes enter the main stream of American art' when the United States Information Service decided in 1958 that they had done so. The art of American Negroes has always been a minority art in the main stream of American culture. It is a continuity without birthdays. It began when the American Negroes emerged as a group and it will continue as long as they think of themselves as a group, which they will do for generations after they are full partners in their native democracy.

Knowing this, most Negro artists are unimpressed by the feathered phrases of escape that periodically float from Hale Woodruff's nest in Washington Square. They do not think of themselves 'simply as American artists', whose primary tasks are to seek fuller 'integration in American life' and identification with 'mid-twentieth century internationalism'.

They regard themselves as Negro artists who are also American artists. They intend to rise *with* their people, not away from them; and so they want their work, through widening and deepening of their artist-audience relationships, to aid a great struggle for deserved satisfactions and fulfilment.

There are, of course, opposing pressures. Well-meaning white friends advise them to move, having come of age, into a larger welcoming fraternity, bound by 'the same ideals and the same characteristics which exist', according to Walter Pach, 'among *all* groups of Americans'. The Mock-Turtle in *Alice* might have had this situation in mind when he sang, 'very slowly and sadly':

See how eagerly the lobsters and the turtles all advance!
They are waiting on the shingle—will you come and join the dance? . . .
You can really have no notion how delightful it will be
When they take us up and throw us, with the lobsters, out to sea!
But the snail replied 'Too far, too far!' and gave a look askance—
Said he thanked the whiting kindly, but he would not join the dance.
Would not, could not, would not, could not, could not join the dance.

The majority of Negro artists have remained as resistant as the snail to alluring advances. Perhaps they are suspicious of the American whiting, perhaps they do not relish the prospect of being thrown out to sea with the lobsters; but their attitude arises mostly from the certainty that they can enrich American art, and thereby merit consideration in world art, by the imaginative cultivation of their own little plots.

Theirs is a sureness which needs no supporting parallels, but it should not be out of place to recall one. The loving vision of Stanley Spencer, probing creatively and physically in the village of his birth, made him a painter whose intense localization turned into a universality extending far beyond sophisticated art-appreciation in the West. Had Spencer painted twins they would have been Mary and Jane Smith of Cookham in Berkshire, but the picture would have been a statement on a phenomenon of universal interest. Rex Goreleigh achieves just that with his conspicuously black *Twins* (plate 36).

In fact, no artist has ever been limited by communal loyalty, by looking with love on his brother's face. The width of an artist's creativeness is not demonstrated by his versatility. It is proportionate to the depth of his roots, absorptive capacity, transforming imaginative power, and technical mastery; and all these qualities gain force from passion.

Malvin Gray Johnson's brief career illustrates this truth. Circumstances kept him mostly in New York, but he worked towards revealing the beauty and tragedy, the colour and aridity, of the Deep South in which he was born. Part of his preparation was technical. First he modified his academic manner to make it more suitable to his purpose; and then he rejected it altogether to create a style of his own based on a study of Impressionism, many experiments with light, colour and form, and close attention to the lessons of African sculpture.

The arresting portraits, genre pictures and visualizations of the spirituals which he painted during this period testify to the successful focusing of his painter's eye; but all are eclipsed by the vitality of the pictures he made in Brightwood, Virginia, in the late summer of 1934. He thought of them as the beginning of his life's work, but they remain the eloquent conclusion of a grand purpose; for he died suddenly in October of the same year.

William Johnson also reached his peak by returning home, though his return was unpremeditated. He was a vagabond painter who spent most of his working life in Europe, especially France, Denmark and Norway. In France, he developed a style, probably derived as much from early exercises in copying cartoons as from Soutine or Munch, which can be called Expressionist; and in Denmark and Norway,

where he more or less settled with Holcha Krake, he carried it nearer to the primitive.

Kerteminde brought him the intimacy of adoption and his painting benefited accordingly (plate 63), but even there he remained an itinerant in search of new experiences. Responding as a Romantic, he put

Irene Clark   *Playmates*

on canvas what excited him visually, or what he liked, but he never looked at Europe with the eye of an indigène. 'There is something in the nature of his forms and lines,' said Pola Gauguin, 'which has great original charm and is a definite expression of a viewpoint and perception very much different from those of the European. . . .' It was this difference that attracted European acclaim. It was the Negro artist, working in a 'Nordic' environment in partial imitation of a way that is characteristically European, that excited interest—a passing interest in novelty which has not raised William Johnson to any status in European art.

On the other hand, when the certainty of war sent Mr and Mrs Johnson to New York in 1938, he built a lasting reputation as a Negro artist and an 'American modern' within seven years. Thinking of himself as a Negro artist, painting for his people at a difficult time, he knew from the start that Expressionism would not suit his purpose. He turned primitive almost at once: primitives were popular and he was already more than inclined in that direction.

Some Negroes did not like the change, for some Negroes like nothing less than Negritude, but the imaginative fervour, dignified simplicity and intimate folk-feeling of William Johnson's genre pictures of Negro life, religious and secular, should secure them a place in world appreciation. They are complimented by the adjectives of outraged genteelity: brutal, distorted, crude, caricatural, odd.

Jesus and the Three Marys (plate 11) is the most 'brutal' of them all. But is its dark brown Jesus (facially an indifferent self-portrait), nailed through enormous, all-embracing hands to a blue cross, and its desolated Marys in orange, light blue and white, anything more than a symbolization of Negro suffering? It has no comparisons in Christian art, but perhaps it is a measure of its suggestiveness that it has recalled the Isenheim altarpiece of 'Grunewald'!

When William Johnson returned to New York, Jacob Lawrence was emerging as another vigorous primitive by intention. By 1941, when he was twenty-four, he had already completed, apart from a number of genre pictures, an amazing series of historical novels in tempera or gouache on small composition boards: *The Life of Toussaint L'Ouverture*, 41 panels; *The Life of Frederic Douglass*, 40 panels; *The Life of Harriet Tubman*, 40 panels; and *The Migration of the Negro Northwards*, 60 panels. To these he quickly added sparkling groups of impressions of Harlem and the War, as well as another historical novel: *The Life of John Brown*.

His work since 1950 includes genre pictures and a series on the Theatre (1952), but it has not been possible to find out exactly what he is doing—his contribution to an exhibition of 1956 was confined to panels from his War series of 1947. Ralph Pearson (1954) recorded him as saying that he wanted 'to grow into the universal, to have the picture bigger in content, to gain a much bigger statement when complete'; but Selden Rodman's interview with him in 1957 indicates that by universality he did not mean more than widening his perspectives as a Negro artist.

Further news of Jacob Lawrence's successes—Rodman found him working on a series on the American Revolution and its long aftermath—would be welcome. Meanwhile, he must be honoured as a unique episodic painter, whose penetrating originality, grasp of content, and terse economy of flat, but essentially three-dimensional, vividly coloured shapes gives his earlier pictures an insistent claim to international consideration. It should be understood, however, that they are illustrations in need of publication with extended captions and knowledgeable introductory essays of literary quality. Almost certainly, Mr Lawrence would then find himself as universal as he hopes to be.

Many other Negro artists have followed William Johnson and Jacob Lawrence in employing a manner that can be called primitive, though distinctively their own: Irene Clark, Claude Clark and Ellis Wilson are amongst the most notable of these neo-primitives of the last few years. Genuine primitives are fewer, for all are exposed to some degree of influence, and without a representative who can be compared with Horace Pippin. According to Selden Rodman (1947) he has no American rival:

Among the self-taught painters of the world, Pippin ranks close to Rousseau, and in the company of Bombois, Peyronnet and Hyppolite. Among American popular masters he is without a rival. . . . Pippin, in contrast to other Americans, has given us a world: sometimes sombre and terrifying, but more often vibrant with counterpoint of textures and ringing colour. And in thirty or forty of the seventy-five oils that he finished in the last six years of his life he managed somehow to convey a vision of the 'American scene'—its history and folklore, its exterior splendour and interior pathos. . . . If there is any conclusion, other than wonder and thankfulness, to be drawn from this phenomenon of Pippin's artistic maturity, it is that the well-springs of art, in America as elsewhere, run much deeper than any of the 'schools' or incestuous fashions would indicate.

Mr Rodman is an authority on folk art whose judgement must be respected. An amateur must accordingly ask his indulgence towards the more cautious admission—quite possibly an underestimate—that Pippin's vision, sensitiveness, dramatic power, precision, unerring feeling for composition, and exuberant use of colour certainly put him in the company of the great American primitives. Even the few pictures we have reproduced prove that.

The same section of plates includes a small selection from the works of some recent self-taught or partly trained Negro artists. Unfortunately, we have not been able to represent Alfredus Williams, who took up painting at sixty-five and showed some magnificent landscapes at the Jo Marino Galleries when he was eighty-three (1958); but we do have (plate 13) the first important painting, and a prize-winning one, by Thomas Jefferson Flanagan, who allowed himself the joy of a palette when he was well past sixty, but not quite beyond 'the cares of a large family creeping up as stair-steps'.

We are also without pictures by Clarence Peacock and Inez Mason, a patient in a New York hospital who had a striking still life in the exhibition of American Primitive Art at the Whitechapel Gallery, London, 1955. Compensations of a truly primitive kind are the reproductions of works (p. 71; plates 11, 14, 16) by Cleo Crawford, Frank Rawlings (on a 'wild nature' theme popular with primitives), Leslie Bolling, and the Nashville stonecutter William Edmonson, whose hand was guided by direct 're-vealment from the Lord'. Edmonson's *Preacher* now enjoys the peace of living underneath an apple tree, in a shady glade bordered by privet hedges, in the garden of R. Lynn Baker's home at East Hampton, Long Island. A limestone cleric could ask no more.

James Washington of Seattle (plate 15) is not really a primitive, for he has had instruction from Mark Tobey, Rivera and Siqueiros, but his paintings have the primitive's unfaltering flatness, vision and unity. His sculptures, based on 'found objects', carry his belief in simplicity to a charming extreme, the birds being specially notable.

John Robinson is a cook in Washington who had the advantage, as a boy, of a few lessons from James Porter. His primitive-like precision, family devotion and joy in life are seen in the three pictures reproduced (plates 12, 13), but it is as a meticulously realistic landscapist that he rises to a stature seldom seen today. For, as Sir Kenneth Clarke says in *Landscape into Art*, 'Realistic landscape, which the ignorant believe to be one of the easiest forms of painting, is actually one of the most inaccessible, one in which success is rarest and most precarious.' Mr Robinson has had pictures in the Barnett Aden Gallery, but Alonzo Aden has still to give him a one-man show which will start him on the road to national recognition. It would be a rewarding effort.

Jewel Simon is one of those phenomenal bundles of good-looking energy who paint, sculpt, write,

Aaron Douglas   *Student*
Mr Douglas continues his vast documentation of the Negro personality

design and make clothes, take part in every neighbourhood activity from church fairs to amateur theatricals, and make a happy home for a delightful family. She has won several prizes in Atlanta University's Art Exhibitions and has grown more sophisticated with each success, but we have wilfully selected one of her older pictures (plate 14) as being most typical of her attitude to life. It is the growth of this attitude, this overwhelming urge to create beauty and extend enjoyment, that warms the climate of appreciation to the point where good art and beautiful things flourish.

Fortunately, there are equally possessed people in every walk of Negro life from the humblest to the highest. Those, for example, who have eaten Aubrey Pankey's Blue Ribbon cooking, surrounded by the paintings, furniture and other works of his own hands, wonder how it is that he is also so distinguished a singer, composer and teacher. He is a photographer, too, but photographing paintings seems to be a skill he has yet to acquire. At any rate, none of the photographs he sent for this book did sufficient justice to the originals to justify reproduction.

Our disappointment at excluding Mr Pankey extends to other Negro painters in his profession, notably Eugene Burkes, Albert Alexander Smith and Leonard Cooper; and to two dancers, Frank Neal and Geoffrey Holder, who are now at least equally well known by their canvases. It is no less regrettable that several self-taught artists of the past, especially John Henry Adams (a teacher who published many

Hale Woodruff   *Courtesy*
Boy 1939   *USIS*
Consciousness of design does not impede the deeply moving quality
of this painting

drawings of the New Negro twenty years before
Alain Locke's book), Henry Avery, William Cooper,
Otis Galbreath (a chauffeur), Vertis Hayes, John
Hailstalk (a laundryman) and Benjamin Kitchin, are
not included—but a book has its limitations.

There is, however, a picture by Edward Loper
(plate 44), a landscapist who reveals more than a
scene; by Samuel Middleton (plate 86), who seems
to be reviving interest in the passé collage; and by
Thomas Sills (plate 91), an ex-labourer whose original
symphonies of form and colour began to find brush-
less orchestration in 1953, when he was nearly forty,
through the inspiration of his wife, Jeanne Reynal,
an artist deservedly praised for her mosaics.

In more formal fields of painting, the leading
associates of the Negro Renaissance and the fertiliz-
ing Decade have added durability to competence.
Some are dead, some are still active, but all will be
gratefully remembered in the history of Negro art:
William Carter, Allan Crite, Elmer Brown, Samuel
Brown, John Hardrick, Edwin Harleston, Palmer
Hayden, Romeyn Van Vleck Lippman, George Neal,
William Edouard Scott and Laura Wheeler Waring
in particular.

The pioneers of the period are still scaling the
peaks. Aaron Douglas continues his vast documentation of the Negro personality (which he should
collect and present) and his irresistible landscapes

and genre pictures. Archibald Motley has shown the
Mexicans a kindred spirit in social understanding,
bold composition and brilliant colour. James Porter
has expanded the combination of characterization
and agreeable decorativeness promised by his early
work. Allan Freelon and Rex Goreleigh are as fresh
and youthful as they were thirty years ago.

Hale Woodruff's compulsive gift for design has
lost none of its vitality, though he has changed its
directions, through his many duties as Professor of
Art Education at New York University. Design is,
in fact, the key word which explains all Mr Woodruff's prints and paintings. Those who thought his
stories of the Negro scene came from a genius inflamed by social awareness should look at them again
with the key word in mind. Design makes sometimes
grotesque stereotypes of many of his characters; it
gives his *Girls Skipping* (plate 82) no more than the
usual charm of his anecdotes; it obscures the mes-
sage of his lynching block print, *Giddap* (1938), to the
point where a tender spinster can miss its horror;
and even in the superb *Amistad* murals it would be
overwhelming were it not for the variety of pose and
expression, captured with masterly draughtsmanship, that lifts them up to the company of the great
wall paintings of today. It may be, therefore, that
the man who made the Atlanta School has been wise
in confining himself recently to charming essays in
'pure aesthetics'.

Apart from the pioneers, those who caught the
discerning eye of Alain Locke in the late 'thirties now
form a galaxy in which the brightest stars are Hughie
Lee-Smith, Eldzier Cortor, Charles Sebree, Romare
Bearden and Charles White. Lee-Smith's penetrating,
but quietly painted, statements on urban desolation
and transition are so true of city life anywhere in the
West that he must be regarded as an artist of world
significance. Cortor, though concerned with the
person rather than the scene, in an exotic and quite
incomparable way, is equally important internationally as a poet of poignancy. Sebree is as bare, almost
medieval, as Cortor is colourful and modern; but the
impact of his studies in contemplation is remarkably
similar. History looks through the eyes of his
women.

Romare Bearden is difficult to assess. He is, in the
best sense, an obsessed painter, moving in widening
circles around the circumstance of being a Negro
persistently devoted to the causes of Negro art.
His early paintings were those of a social realist with
a difference, the difference being an expressionist
toughness suited to the mood and conditions of the
'thirties. At much the same time, he produced
several beautiful, purely decorative water colours
which hinted at developments in another direction.

Lois Mailou Jones
Old Street in Montmartre

Courtesy Mr and Mrs Albert S. Gerstein,
Design (*Columbus, Ohio*) *and the Artist*

They came in what was a transformed combination of the two tendencies, for out of his Negro experience, and his inclination to master colour and flat, near-abstract design, there grew a series of plangent constructions reaching out to the common denominators that touch all men, as indicated by the titles of three principal groups of pictures: *The Passion of Christ*, *The Joy of Life* (Rabelais), and *The Death of the Bullfighter* (Lorca).

Photographs suggest that the tensions of movement and colour were not always resolved in these semi-abstractions, yet they inspire confidence in an ultimate fusion of intention and technique which would definitely place Mr Bearden with the great modern artists. In 1959 the fusion seemed to be still in the making—at least so he more or less says himself:

> I have not had a one-man show since 1955, but I have been working hard on new paintings. They are difficult to describe: austere in colour, a very flat plane, a shallow space, and in some aspects near the old Chinese paintings, but without representational elements. I am, naturally, very interested in form and structure—in a personal way of expression which can perhaps be called new. I have nothing, of course, against representational images, but the demands, the direction, of the sign factors in my painting now completely obliterate any representational image. . . . I am trying to find out what there is in me that is common to, or touches, other men. It is hard to do and realize.

Happily Mr Bearden has since had an exhibition at the Michael Warren Gallery, New York, which suggests that he has achieved what he has pursued for so long. Stuart Preston of the *New York Times* (23.1.60) described what he saw as the work of 'a virtuoso of texture and of sumptuous and subtle colour if ever there was one'. Carlyle Burrows of the *Herald Tribune* (24.1.60) responded as follows:

> That which materialises is not specific but remote and poetic . . . a sublimation of private experiences more than realisations of communicable subject matter. Forms and colours seem filtered into canvases, gaining remarkable hues and textures as though they were strained through a sieve. Greys and quiet brick reds and blues are used, with the luminosity of the colour of an insect's wing, or the flaring form of a lovely flower.

Charles White is a painter by the right of having raised drawing, with conte crayon or Chinese ink, to the level of painting. He is also a preacher, but a preacher so inspiring and searchingly eloquent that people of all faiths and nations have been uplifted by him. Indeed, his power has made the necessary

Eldzier Cortor
Two Figures on Bed
Courtesy University of Illinois

exclusion of several of his pictures from this book the most distressing trial in its preparation. It is relieved by letting him state his philosophy:

> The substance of man is such that he has to satisfy the needs of life with all his senses. His very being cries out for these senses to appropriate the true riches of life: the beauty of human relationships and dignity, of nature and art, realized in striding towards a bright tomorrow. . . . Without culture, without creative art, inspiring to these senses, mankind stumbles in a chasm of despair and pessimism. . . .

> My work takes shape around images and ideas that are centred within the vortex of the life experience of a Negro. . . . I look to life and to my people as the founthead of challenging ideas and monumental concepts. I look to Rembrandt, Goya, Daumier, Kollwitz, Orosco, Gatuso for greater knowledge of craft. I look for security in alliance with the *millions* of artists throughout the world with whom I share common goals, And I look to all mankind to communicate with and to appropriate my works.

Humility in his presence, and pride in possessing

Charles White
Mahalia Jackson
Courtesy Harry Belafonte

49

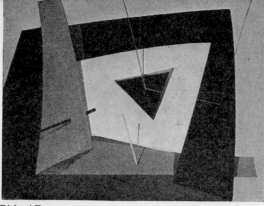

Richard Dempsey
Planes and Lines

*Courtesy
the Artist*

him, repel learned-looking asides on his 'sweep and strength', massive sculpturing, unmatched draughtsmanship and influences. These are evident anyway and are just as evidently subordinate to his purpose. On the achievement of that purpose another great artist, Harry Belafonte, writes eloquently:

> There is a powerful, sometimes violent, beauty in his artistic interpretation of Negro Americans. There is the poetic beauty of Negro idiom. This is his most profound contribution, and it is significant that his art has never strayed far from the roots which gave birth to the artist himself. In a period when many artists have deserted reality . . . Mr White has continued to work for broader horizons of human expression and to explore deeper dimensions of truth and reality. . . . His strokes are bold and courageous and affirmative. His lines are clear, his people are alive with a zest for life and the story of living manifest in their faces and bodies . . . his people take on a reality all their own. You feel that somewhere sometime some place you have known these people before or will meet them somewhere along life's journey. You are enriched by the experience of having known Charles White's people, who are like characters from a great novel that remain with you long after the pages of the book have been closed.

Lois Mailou Jones is the only woman who belongs in this company. She has experimented interestingly, but she remains an artist without pretensions. She is a lovable painter because she loves the people and places she paints: they are never 'subjects'. This quality is happily reflected in snapshots, sent by one of our 'spies', of her in France. Surrounded by children and adults, she neither ignores them nor seeks their attention. She goes on working *with* them. If a brush stroke goes wrong and she makes a *moue*, their faces are contorted in silent sympathy; she puts it right and they smile with relieved approval.

This encompassing love makes her genre portrait of *Jennie* (plate 38) a long story of human qualities in a single canvas; and it shows, of course, in all her other work. For the same reason, she becomes de-

lightfully French in France. She enjoys herself hugely and shares her pleasure with us, but as we look the thought grows that the whole underprivileged world deserves such beauty. A painter who communicates like that is a major 'social realist' too.

Many more Negro artists of the 'thirties have reached national distinction. Charles Alston, a fertilizing teacher, seems to be as versatile as ever. Ernest Crichlow has matured his early sympathy with childhood, adolescence and motherhood in a deeply stirring way. Lena Horne, who first saw one of his pictures in a group exhibition, records a widely shared response:

> I was instantly drawn to it. It was a picture of a little girl crouched on a battered stairway looking out at the world with infinite hope, her eyes still unclouded by doubt. I am happy to say that now . . . I can look into her serene eyes as often as I want and need to.

Norman Lewis has moved from sympathetic, but often witty, concern with Harlem to representational or abstract designs of immediate feminine charm and evocative quality. Often, it has rightly been said, they are 'poetic hieroglyphs'. Beauford DeLaney, 'the amazing and invariable' bohemian of Henry Miller's doxology of blood and race, has left Greene Street for Paris, and colourful commentaries for the purities of paint and form. His compositions are so integrated, suggestive and captivating that they rouse the feeling, impeded by regard for words, that there is paint in his soul. Indeed, genetic magic would allow one to agree that he was 'an artist in the womb, and even before that'.

Mr DeLaney's compositions, such as the delightful *Composition Jaune* (1958), are designed harmonies, as are those of Joseph Grey and Edwin Lewis; but those of William Compton seem to be more 'interior' and exuberant—he has exhibited with Action Painters. The future of these young men will certainly be watched with interest.

The slightly older 'emancipated Negro artists' appear to have been content with lesser degrees of emancipation. Their leaders—Richard Dempsey, Delilah Pierce, Walter Simon, Merton Simpson and Alma Thomas—are abstractionists in the old-fashioned sense of abstracting a subject. They do it interestingly, as our few pictures show, and with a working regard for the promotion of Negro art as a whole. Miss Thomas, for example, is a Vice-President of the Barnett Aden Gallery. Walter Simon, whose East Indian father was comforted by his son's success as a portrait painter at the age of ten, has a workaday philosophy of art reflected in his invariable introduction (printed by Reddick) to the exhibi-

50

Walter Simon   *Looking Over the Fence*

tions he arranges for summer school students who are junior school teachers:

> This exhibition is proof of the fact that all people are capable of expressing themselves artistically.
>
> These are not 'works of art'. . . . Education in a democracy is not primarily concerned with developing 'great art' or artists. Rather, it should be concerned with helping the 'average' student further to develop his sensitivities, which education in the past has tended to deaden and frustrate instead of broadening and enriching.

Most of the younger artists remain, as the older ones do, representational or expressively symbolic. They want to communicate. 'The essence of painting for me', writes Leedell Moorehead, 'is the crystallization and communication of ideas. The artist must communicate. Otherwise, for whom is he painting?' Phillip Hampton extends this view:

> A work of art is a visual philosophy, a non-verbal communication; for art is a combining process of the biological environment and spiritual constituents in the totality of man.
>
> Therefore, if an artist is to produce a work of art, he must be acutely sensitive to the totality. He must not be bound by the procedures of cold analysis for which, in many cases, he has been trained. His is the very difficult task of combining, juxtaposing, thinking, disposing of, sensing and otherwise creating . . . the phenomenon termed art. It is a catharsis of his own individuality. When I have completed a picture, I know immediately whether I have portrayed my total feelings, or whether I have been bound by an intellectual façade. . . . Evidently, I am still seeking this ideal of totality. . . .
>
> American Negro artists need the recognition and greater understanding that surveys of their work should bring. It is only through recognition *as a group* that we will eventually become known as artists who are incidentally Negroes.

Unfortunately, this book is not a survey. It is only a restricted sampling, especially in so far as the younger painters are concerned. But it does show

something of their range and purpose, from the gripping realism of John Biggers, John Wilson and James Reuben Reed to the semi-abstractions and abstractions of Eugene Grigsby, Mildred Thompson and Roosevelt Woods.

Many of the youngest have still to be proved by time, a force so eliminating in underprivileged groups that a distressing number of talents fail to survive from one decade to the next. It is reasonably certain, however, that those represented in the plates are climbing the ladder to lasting distinction; and so are some whose pictures, for various reasons, we have failed to show. Among them Frank Alston, John Arterberry, Mildred Braxton, Benjamin Britt, Sylvester Britton, Nicholas Canyon, Ladybird Cleveland, Virginia Cox, Harvey Cropper, Leroy Foster, Thomas Harris, Yvonne Hunt, Clifford Jackson, Paul Keene, Leon Leonard and Percy Ricks will surely have prominent places in a later book on American Negro art.

The painters cannot be left without directing special attention to four youngish men whose firm

Merton Simpson   *Nude*

51

regional reputations are spreading over the continent: Humbert Howard of Philadelphia, Walter Sanford and Stan Williamson of Chicago, and Alvin Hollingsworth of New York. Howard thinks of his 'work as an evolution of personal discovery and experience' and we profit from his deep understanding through beautifully patterned interpretations of exceptional clarity, force and elegance.

Sanford is a charmer, whether in his shrewd, expressionist semi-abstracts or in scenic abstractions that seldom protest if they are looked at vertically instead of horizontally. The point he makes is always taken: roused to pungency by one of his most economic character studies, *The New York Times Book Review* (21 September 1958) printed it with the caption, 'a prolonged agony of dissimulation'.

Williamson is a landscapist, pictorial calligrapher, book illustrator and art director of a publishing company. His paintings of old houses in Chicago, and his calligraphic still lifes, never fail to vibrate chords of pleasure, but he must settle. When he does America will have another great painter, perhaps mostly of the dignity that has resisted progress.

Hollingsworth represents an increasing return from refining forms and pigments to the pressing claims and complications of modern life. He demands quotation:

In some circles it is almost a crime to paint figurative work. To organize a composition around the figure or any recognizable subject allegedly detracts from its artistic quality. Although subject matter is again entering the contemporary art scene, a tremendous wealth of themes remains ignored . . . I have painted in both fashions—figuratively and abstractly. . . . After working abstractly, I had a dual reason for again attacking subject matter with renewed vigour. First, I recognized I should take advantage of themes close to me. Secondly, I felt there should be some fusion of my figurative experience with my abstract experiences with colour. The result has been that the conflicts of techniques and schools no longer exist for me. The abstract fuses with the figurative in my work. . . .

The people of the beat generation and their emotions have brought about in me a compulsion to paint them in a series of configurations of actions and attitudes. I use figurative means if I feel they will help me to say what I want to say dynamically. But when I approach the expression of feelings, moods and sensual diversions, I find that abstract painting yields a more suitable creative tool. Expression is the first consideration; and the artist must assert the right, as Picasso has done, to express himself as he sees fit and in whatever way he feels at the time.

The absence of pictures supporting this viewpoint

Phillip Hampton
Class Drawing

*Courtesy
the Artist*

has been another of the frustrations attending this book. Photographs of Mr Hollingsworth's *Beat Scene* series, and of his remarkable line-simple drawings in Harlem, were not available in time for publication; but the little we have shown of his work points to the eye, style and social involvements of an internationally significant artist.

Coming to the print makers, the high standards created by the stimuli of the Roosevelt Era, and the teaching of Allan Freelon, James Lesesne Wells and Hale Woodruff, have been maintained but not surpassed, except by Charles White. Those who became prominent then, especially Robert Blackburn and Wilmer Jennings, are still the leaders and James Wells remains their 'dean'; but it is a decade or so since Margaret Taylor Burroughs, Elizabeth Catlett, Frederic Jones and John Wilson were admitted to their circle. Dox Thrash continues in his versatile and striking way with prints made by the carborundum process invented by himself.

Birds of passage from painting to printmaking are, of course, numerous and frequently very successful. In the recent exhibition of *American Prints Today*, Walter Williams attracted special attention with his *Fighting Cock* (plate 90), a large colour woodcut on a recurrent theme in his much admired paintings. Gustav von Groschwitz, a pioneer in the popularization of American printmaking, says of it that 'The apprehensive boy, and the cock full of fight, the rural setting and large areas of red and black, convey a naiveté that tends to obscure the very skilful cutting of the blocks of this print which has a refreshing directness.'

Norma Morgan is a regular migrant who stays perhaps a little longer in the world of printmaking and drawing than in that of painting. A measure of her technique and patient capacity for detail is a table setting, *Glass and Silver*, done in tempera when she was nineteen, of a perfection seldom seen today. She has two consuming interests: 'wild love', which her sentimentality reduces to sylvan fun and games; and the fantasy landscape, which can seldom be convincing in an age when it arises from intellection and not, as in the days of the old masters, from belief. Her fascination for rock patterns comes, directly or indirectly, from Leonardo da Vinci, who advised the painter to:

> ... look at certain walls stained with damp or at stones of uneven colour. If you have to invent some setting you will be able to see in these the likeness of divine landscapes, adorned with mountains, ruins, rocks, woods, great plains, hills and valleys in great variety; and then again you will see there battles and strange figures in violent action, expressions of faces and clothes, and an infinity of things which you will be able to reduce to their complete and proper forms.

By looking in this way at 'a confusion of shapes the spirit is quickened to *new inventions*'. Miss Morgan's spirit is quickened into materializing ethereal shapes, but without benefit of local childhood memories and extensive reading. Unfamiliarity with the 'little people', who 'Travell much Abroad' without change in their national 'Apparell and Speech', is evident in her inclination to show them as Boris Karloffish giants dressed by the standards of theatrical fancy. Odder still is her portrait of an exceptionally itinerant kelpie, which she saw winking at her on the Yorkshire moors. The drawing could have been presented as a semi-abstract study of Farmer Brown's pixolated small boy, but its excellence confirms the impression that art will gain if Miss Morgan acquires thematic control.

Little can be said of Negro achievements in illustration. In straightforward drawing, Charles White and Elton Fax, whose 'chalk talks' are deservedly popular, have few rivals anywhere; but our text pictures also suggest that a wealth of talent awaits full entry into such fields as book illustration and visual reportage. It will be best used when it is understood that artistic opportunities to collaborate with Negro writers, such as Arna Bontemps, who touch the innerness of Negro life belong by right to those who are in it. Feliks Topolski, who has illustrated Mr Bontemps' *Lonesome Road*, will be the first to admit this when he thinks about it.

Pictorial journalism is beyond the province of this book, but a passing tribute must be paid to Ollie Harrington and Elmer Simms Campbell. Mr Harrington's crisply drawn cartoons can now be enjoyed in book form, but Mr Arnold Gingrich of *Esquire*

Robert Blackburn   *Courtesy*
Boy with Green Head   *Atlanta Univ.*

has yet to give us a volume which will be a worthy compliment to a gay, vital and humanistic artist. It would be an event. For Mr Campbell's range in pen and ink, pencil and colours extends from Negro genre, scenes in Haiti and brilliant imitations of the Fauves, to the globular blondes and lecherous pashas which devotees of *Esquire* know so well.

Finally, we come to the sculptors. American Negro sculpture is so good and extensive that only a bare sampling, and very little selection, has been possible. The pioneers of the Negro Renaissance,

Frederic Jones   *Courtesy*
Magnolia Seed   *I.B.M.*

Norma Morgan
Middle Dene Farm

*Courtesy Associated
American Artists N.Y.*

and their rivals in the 'thirties, remain at the top, with Richmond Barthé on a pinnacle of international fame by himself. Barthé's sculpture, whether small or heroic, is immense with the 'immensity of life'.

Augusta Savage, William Artis and Joseph Kersey share the same gift for communication of ideas and intensities in an unmannered way that often recalls the best Hellenistic studies of Africans. One of these is the bronze head, illustrated in the frontispiece to *A Coat of Many Colours*, which Herbert Read calls 'the greatest work of art in the world'. Only two inches high, it 'stood among a crowd of small objects, unlabelled and unhonoured', in the Museo Archaeologico at Florence, but 'it seemed to shine there like a glow-worm in the darkness of my mood'.

Still more moving is the wistful bronze head, four inches high, of an African girl (or boy) recently described and illustrated by D. E. L. Haynes of the British Museum. It was probably made in Alexandria between 300 and 100 B.C. and is the work of a sculptor of Greek culture, though not necessarily of Greek origin. There is nothing comparable in Graeco-Roman sculpture, or among the Benin and Ife bronzes it anticipates; and photographs of it, which can be bought from the British Museum, should be available in every Negro institution concerned with art.

Age lends an aura to these two exquisite pieces, but proper reverence for them should increase appreciation of the classical quality in Barthé, Artis and some other Negro sculptors. More than 'deepest questionings' or sensitively 'subdued pathos', they sometimes concentrate all Negro history, potentiality and hope in a single quietly alive work—as Barthé does in *The Negro Looks Ahead*. Universally appeal-

ing, it looks forward from a long yesterday to all the tomorrows, clouded and bright, of the coloured peoples everywhere.

Sargent Johnson touches the same chords in his own versatile, and frequently polychrome, way; and so does Henry Bannarn in his less mannered moments. Among the more conscious social realists, Elizabeth Catlett and Marion Perkins never fail to charge their picture-making sculptures with depths of emotion that flood the mind in successive waves. The attitude of the group they lead is unequivocally stated by Miss Catlett:

I believe that art should be available to all people. Non-objective art, for me, has many valuable aesthetic qualities, but has been used to create a snob group in the arts, both of creators and observers. Magazine cover and calendar art, on the other hand, has been used to dull the natural aesthetic feelings of ordinary people. Here, in Mexico, it is different. There is a rich historical tradition in art; and the poorer people, who are great creators in the popular arts, regularly visit the murals and museums. Their appreciation extends to all art forms that do not require special and formal education to be understood.

Miss Catlett is proudly claimed as an alumnus by the University of Iowa. The vitality of its Art Department has also benefited Ed Wilson, whose humanistic and patriotic involvements are carved into everything he has done. A great future belongs to him, but the present leaves him so isolated in Durham, North Carolina, that he feels it 'is tantamount to my not existing locally as an artist'. The world of Hale Woodruff, in which there is no need for 'special efforts' on behalf of Negro art and artists because 'practically all avenues of opportunity are

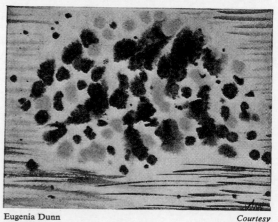

Eugenia Dunn
Encore

*Courtesy
Amanda Bailey*

An experiment in composition and colours—dropped with a pipette and blotted

54

Ellis Wilson
Marchande
Special photograph
for this book by
Carl Van Vechten

open to (them) as they are open to all' is not even a dream world to him.

His convictions are based on realities; and he is 'more than convinced that there is strong need for the Negro artist to be represented and to represent his people.' Appalled by 'the decline in communicable content', and emphasis on 'arbitrary revolts or personal uniqueness', it is his 'intention to proceed in the hope of extracting content from life and re-creating it in sculpture with formal and psychological values readily discernible to the eye and mind'. A 'logical tradition, developed by broad integration within the humanities', is inseparable, he says, from this purpose.

Carroll Simms, like his colleague John Biggers (a considerable sculptor as well as a painter), belongs with the social realists who seek the larger integration of the arts; and so do Gregory Ridley and Hayward Oubré. Simms is already a major figure; Ridley, who says there is 'nothing extraordinary' about his progress since he left Fisk University ten years ago, has moved, with his painting associate Harper Phillips, into neo-primitivism; Oubré's versatility, encouraged perhaps by the need to work demonstratively with his students, might find its best expression, both humorous and serious, in sculpture.

Barbara Chase, Richard Hunt, Carroll Simms and Jack Jordan lead the plates on sculpture, because we have felt that Richmond Barthé and Sargent Johnson, who need no 'placing', would wish to give way to these newcomers. Few young sculptors anywhere promise more than they do. Jordan, like Simms, has

Hayward Oubré
Self-Portrait

*Courtesy
Atlanta Univ.*

much to say; Barbara Chase's inflammatory interest in bulls and bullfighters has as its other aspect the customary pieties; Richard Hunt is scientifically intent on solving problems. He can afford to do so.

An early definition—he was then twenty-two—of Mr Hunt's approach was prepared for the Museum of Modern Art when it purchased his *Arachne* in 1957. In it the ivory tower of the greybeards becomes the mousetrap of post-war youth:

> To a great extent the success of an artist in to-day's society might still be a matter of building a better mousetrap. There is danger in being drawn into the whirlpool of day-to-day relations. In this respect, the problem is to keep one's head in the clouds but one's feet on the ground. I think that artists who posit as a first condition of a contemporary culture the fostering of art dream in vain and ask too much. To work in relative freedom within its complicated framework is enough.
>
> Out of a number of possible bases for judging art the dominance of the style peculiar to any given period always makes one basis more tenable than the rest; but this one criterion is always tempered by the prevailing intellectual and social climate. . . . Thus, the critical basis of art is as everchanging as the works it seeks to evaluate. . . .
>
> It seems to me that the seeds of artistic revolution sown, grown and reaped during the last fifty years should see the rich fruits of their harvest nurture a new art in this wiser half century—an art

Hayward Oubré
Young Horse

Courtesy the Artist
WIRE

55

which need not seek strength in revolt, but in the creative pulse of its makers; an art having sinew and gut as well as heart and soft flesh.

This persuasive philosophy of acceptance is not altogether in keeping with the vertical extension required by keeping one's head damp in the clouds, but it reconciles easily with 'increasingly expansive' treatment of steel and space. Mr Hunt's purpose is to get:

... strong three-dimensional statements: to use every element of tri-dimensionality in one sculpture—spatial and planar themes projecting into space, solid volumes completely displacing it, and concave or hollow volumes used with the other elements in combinations and multiples to displace and enclose space. Thus, the complications of form are additive and always related to basic units.

Emotional and image conditions are, of course, affected by size, height and spatial positioning. The problem of my sculpture therefore involves the penetration of space by line, plane and volume, as well as the implications of image and emotion.

Comparable clarity of ideas and intentions often indicates a closed mind, but in Mr Hunt it points to growth. He recognizes now that 'the search for clarity often misses the goal'. He has 'turned again to figures, but with interest in more complex relationships within the figure. In *Arachne*, for example, I have tried to show hybrid figures in metamorphosis.' Inevitably, he will 'keep, and pass, and turn again'.

Indeed, he appears to be moving, with Barbara Chase and other young Negro sculptors, towards a concept of significance recently defined by Henry Moore in a conversation with Edouard Roditi:

Sculpture for me must have life in it, vitality. It must have a feeling for organic form, a certain pathos and warmth. Purely abstract sculpture seems to me to be an activity that would be better fulfilled in another art, such as architecture. . . . But sculpture is different from architecture. . . . It should always give the impression, whether carved or modelled, of having grown organically, created by pressure from within.

Admirers of Selma Burke, who is not represented here at her recent best, will soon be pleasured, it is believed, by a book of her work; but those who took pride in Nancy Elizabeth Prophet's successes will have to reconcile themselves to her loss. She writes that 'an anthropologist must certainly know' she is 'not a negro'. Perhaps he does—and a little more as well.

Ceramics, regrettably, must be treated as a postscript. Negro potters are invariably good, and some reach the high standards set by William Artis; but

Richard Hunt   *From a Sketchbook*

Earl Hooks seems to be alone in following the sculptural tradition, without sacrificing function, of the early Negro potters. His vivid transformations of biological shapes have a vigour and movement, increased by the feeling they give of the linked variety of organic growth, suggestive of American Negro art as a whole—properly so, for pottery is an early art and a sure guide to the sensibilities of a people.

This tribute to a master potter, and a dedicated teacher of art, is an agreeable note on which to close a book offering a glimpse, in which much has remained out of focus, of the artistic thinking, struggles, confusions and achievements of a people whose history has no parallel in the modern world. They know, peculiarly, how sharp has been the conquering of the jungle path to each stage of human dignity; and what they show of their knowledge through their art is accordingly of more than universal interest. It is an inspiration.

The Background

Aptheker, Herbert (ed.). 1951. *A Documentary History of the Negro People in the United States.* New York: Citadel Press.

Brown, Sterling, Davis, Arthur and Lee, Ulysses. 1941. *The Negro Caravan.* New York: Dryden. Quoted from pp. 884, 894, 895.

Butcher, Margaret Just and Locke, Alain. 1956. *The Negro in American Culture.* New York: Knopf.

Carava, Roy de and Hughes, Langston. 1955. *The Sweet Flypaper of Life.* New York: Simon and Schuster.

Cunard, Nancy (ed.). 1934. *Negro.* London: Wishart.

Davie, Emily. 1954. *Profile of America.* New York: Crowell.

Davis, John (ed.). 1958. Africa Seen by American Negroes. *Présence Africaine* (Paris), special vol.

Diop, Alioune (ed.). 1956, 57. Le Premier Congrès International des Ecrivains et Artistes Noirs. *Présence Africaine* (Paris), 8–9–10, 1956; 14–15, 1957.

Dover, Cedric. 1937. *Half-Caste.* London: Secker and Warburg.

Dover, Cedric (ed.). 1953. The American Negro. *United Asia* (Bombay), June.

Dover, Cedric. Culture and Creativity. See Diop, Alioune. 1956.

Du Bois, W. E. B. 1935. *Black Reconstruction.* New York: Harcourt.

Du Bois, W. E. B. 1939. *Black Folk Then and Now.* New York: Holt.

Fisher, Miles Mark. 1953. *Negro Slave Songs in the United States.* New York: Cornell Press.

Franklin, John Hope. 1947. *From Slavery to Freedom.* New York: Knopf.

Franklin, John and Logan, Rayford. 1957. Negro, American. *Encyclopaedia Britannica*, 16:194–200. London: Encyclopaedia Britannica.

Frazier, E. Franklin. 1939. *The Negro Family in the United States.* Chicago: University Press. Quoted from p. 412.

Frazier, E. Franklin. 1957. *Race and Culture Contacts in the Modern World.* New York: Knopf.

Frazier, E. Franklin. 1957. *The Negro in the United States.* New York: Macmillan. Quot. from p. 57.

Frazier, E. Franklin. 1957. *Black Bourgeoisie.* Glencoe (Illinois): The Free Press. Quotations from pp. 24, 237.

Frazier, E. Franklin. 1958. Potential American Negro Contributions to African Social Development. See Davis, John.

Gayarré, Charles. Quoted from Frazier, 1957 (Macmillan), p. 77.

Handy, W. C. (ed.). 1926. *A Treasury of the Blues.* New York: Simon and Schuster. Reprinted 1949.

Haynes, D. E. L. 1957. Bronze Bust of a Young Negress. *British Museum Quarterly.* 21(1):21–22, pl. IV.

Herskovits, Melville. 1941. *The Myth of the Negro Past.* New York: Harper.

Homer, Dorothy and Robinson, Evelyn. 1955. *The Negro: A Selected Bibliography.* New York: The New York Public Library.

Hughes, Langston. 1926. *The Weary Blues.* New York: Knopf. Tenth printing, 1945.

Hughes, Langston. 1940. *The Big Sea.* New York: Knopf. Much about the Negro Renaissance.

Hughes, Langston and Bontemps, Arna (eds.). 1949. *The Poetry of the Negro.* New York: Doubleday.

Hughes, Langston and Meltzer, Milton. 1956. *A Pictorial History of the Negro in America.* New York: Crown Publishers.

Hughes, Langston and Bontemps, Arna (eds.). 1958. *The Book of Negro Folklore.* New York: Dodd, Mead.

Isaacs, Edith, J. R. 1947. *The Negro in the American Theatre.* New York: Theatre Arts.

Johnson, Charles (ed.). 1927. *Ebony and Topaz: A Collectanea.* New York: *Opportunity.* Several illustrations by Aaron Douglas.

Johnson, James Weldon, 1922. *The Book of American Negro Poetry.* New York: Harcourt Brace. Revised edition 1931.

Johnson, James Weldon, 1928. The Dilemma of the Negro Author. *American Mercury*, December.

Johnson, James Weldon. 1930. *Black Manhattan.* New York: Knopf.

Johnson, James Weldon and Johnson, J. Rosamund. 1947. *The Book of American Negro Spirituals.* New York: The Viking Press.

Laughlin, Clarence, 1942. *New Orleans and Its Living Past.* Boston: Houghton Mifflin.

Laughlin, Clarence. 1948. *Ghosts Along the Mississippi.* New York: Scribner's.

Lips, Julius. 1937. *The Savage Hits Back or The White Man Through Native Eyes.* London: Lovat Dickson.

Logan, Rayford. 1954. *The Negro in American Life and Thought.* New York: Dial Press.

Logan, Rayford et al. 1955. *The New Negro Thirty Years Afterward (a*

BIBLIOGRAPHY

by Maureen Dover

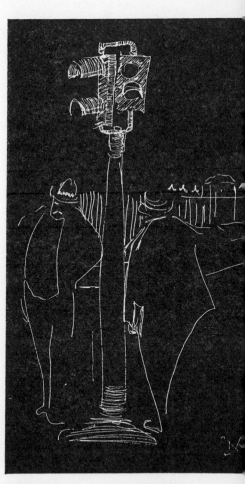

Roland Turner
Street Corner

*Courtesy C.A.G.
New York City*

Memorial to Alain Locke). Washington, D.C.: Howard University Press.

Locke, Alain (ed.). 1924. Harlem: Mecca of the New Negro. *Survey Graphic*, March.

Locke, Alain (ed.). 1925. *The New Negro*. New York: Boni. Several illustrations by Aaron Douglas.

Locke, Alain. 1943. *Le Rôle du Nègre dans la Culture des Amèriques*. Port-au-Prince (Haiti): Government Press.

Locke, Alain, 1944. The Negro in the Three Americas. *Journal of Negro Education*. Winter Number.

McKay, Claude. 1928. *Home to Harlem*. New York: Harper.

McKay, Claude. 1940. *Harlem: Negro Metropolis*. New York: Dutton.

Metropolitan Museum of Art. 1939. *Life in America*. New York.

Monod, Théodore (ed.). 1950. Le Monde Noir. *Présence Africaine* (Paris), 8–9.

Moore, Henry, 1952. The Sculptor in Modern Society. In *International Conference of Artists*. Paris: Unesco. Quotation from p. 102.

Nordholt, J. W. Schulte. 1960. *The People that Walk in Darkness*. London: Burke.

Owens, William. 1953. *Slave Mutiny*. New York: John Day. Story of the *Amistad* mutiny.

Quarles, Benjamin. 1953. *The Negro in the Civil War*. Boston: Little, Brown.

Roditi, Edouard. 1960. *Dialogues on Art*. London: Secker and Warburg. The quotation on p. 160 is from *The Observer*, London, 10 April 1960.

Saxon, Lyle, Dreyer, Edward and Tallant, Robert. 1945. *Gumbo Ya-Ya*. Boston: Houghton Mifflin. Quotations from pp. 216, 219, 227.

Unesco 1951, 53. *Courier*. July–August; October. Children's Art.

Van Vechten, Carl. 1926. *Nigger Heaven*. New York: Knopf.

Walker, Margaret. 1942. *For My People*. New Haven: Yale University Press.

Waxman, Julia. 1945. *Race Relations: A Selected List of Readings*. Chicago: Julius Rosenwald Fund.

American Negro Art

(In this selected list some general books on art are included because they contain brief references to American Negro art. For books on American art see the bibliographies, listed below, by the United States Information Service.)

Adams, John Henry. 1904. The New Negro Woman; The New Negro Man. *Voice of the Negro*, August, October. Historically interesting amateur drawings.

Anon. 1928. Archibald J. Motley Jr. *Opportunity*, April. Reproductions of *Aline—An Octoroon, Waganda Charm Makers, Syncopation* and *A Mulattress*.

Anon. 1941. . . . and the Migrants Kept Coming. *Fortune*, November. Many of Jacob Lawrence's *Migration* series in colour.

Anon. 1946. Negro Artists. *Life*, July 22. Works by Marion Perkins, Eldzier Cortor, Jacob Lawrence, Horace Pippin, Romare Bearden, William Johnson, John Wilson, Palmer Hayden in colour; heads by Richmond Barthé, Sargent Johnson, Eloise Bishop and William Artis in black and white.

Anon. 1950. Nineteen Young American Artists. *Life*, March 20. Cortor's *Room Number Five* in full page colour.

Anon. 1958. Leading Young Artists. *Ebony*, April. The following artists with their pictures: Hughie Lee-Smith, Joseph Grey, Gilbert Harris, Virginia Cox, Paul Keene, Leon Leonard, Charles White, Harvey Cropper, Leroy Foster, Edwin Lewis, Norma Morgan, Sylvester Britton, Artis Lane (in colour); Barbara Chase, Merton Simpson, Clarence Peacock, Walter Williams, Thomas Harris, Nicholas Canyon (in black and white).

Anon. 1958. Oils by Humbert Howard. *Art Alliance Bulletin* (Philadelphia), November.

Anon. 1959. The Art Career of Eugenia Dunn. *The Illustrator* (Minneapolis), Summer.

Atlanta University Art Exhibitions. 1942–60. For descriptive illustrated accounts see *Atlanta Univ. Bull.*, July of each year. The issue for July 1952 also contains an illustrated description of Hale Woodruff's murals on *The Art of the Negro*.

Barr, Alfred (ed.). 1942. *Painting and Sculpture in the Museum of Modern Art*. New York: Museum of Modern Art.

Barthé, Richmond. No date. *Sculpture*. New York: Harmon Foundation. A portfolio.

Bearden, Romare. 1934. The Negro Artist and Modern Art. *Opportunity* (New York), December.

Bier, Justus. 1950. Ellis Wilson. *Courier Journal Magazine*, April 30. Several pictures in colour.

Biggers, John. 1954. *The Negro Woman in American Life and Education: A Mural Presentation*.

Ann Arbor, Michigan: University Microfilms.

Burroughs, Margaret et al. 1959. *National Conference of Negro Artists*. Atlanta: Atlanta University.

Burton, E. Milby. 1942. *South Carolina Silversmiths, 1690–1800*. Charleston Museum, S. Carolina.

Cahill, Holger et al. 1938. *Masters of Popular Painting*. New York: Museum of Modern Art.

Campbell, E. Simms. 1950. *Esquire*, December. Four pictures in colour, in the manner of Van Gogh, Picasso, Renoir and Seurat, on pp. 120–21.

Catlett, Elizabeth. 1944. The Negro Artist in America. *American Contemporary Art*, April.

Cole, Natalie Robinson. 1942. *Arts in the Classroom*. New York: Day.

Crite, Allan. 1944. *Were You There when They Crucified my Lord?* Cambridge (Mass.): Harvard.

Crite, Allan. 1947. *All Glory*. Cambridge (Mass.): Soc. of St. John the Evangelist.

Crite, Allan. 1948. *Is it Nothing to You?* Boston: Episcopal Diocese of Massachusetts.

Crite, Allan. 1948. *Three Spirituals from Earth to Heaven*. Cambridge (Mass.): Harvard.

Daniels, John. 1914. *In Freedom's Birthplace: a Study of Boston Negroes*. Boston: Houghton Mifflin.

Dawson, Charles. 1947. The Negro in Art. *Negro Year Book*, Alabama; Tuskegee Institute. See also 1952 edition.

Desdunes, Rodolph. 1911. *Nos Hommes et Notre Histoire. Notices Biographiques Accompagnées de Reflexion et de Souvenirs Personnels*. Montreal: Arbour and Dupont. Notes on Eugene and Daniel Warbourg and Alexander Pickhil (painter).

Diop, Alioune (ed.). 1951. L'Art Nègre. *Présence Africaine* (Paris), 10, 11.

Douglas, Aaron, 1936. The Negro in American Culture. *First American Artists' Congress*, New York.

E.G. 1959. Ein Broadway-Romantiker Am Zürichsee. *Sie und Er* (Zofingen), No. 31. On E. Simms Campbell.

Finkelstein, Sidney. 1955. *Charles White: Ein Künstler Amerikas*. Dresden: Verlag der Kunst. 43 plates, 1 in colour.

Ford, Alice. 1949. *Pictorial Folk Art: New England to California*. New York: Studio Publications.

Groschwitz, Gustave von. 1959.

American Prints Today. *The Studio*, October.

Hale, R. B. (ed.). 1950. 100 *American Painters of the Twentieth Century*. New York: Metropolitan Museum of Art.

Harmon Foundation. No date. *William H. Johnson, an Artist of the World Scene*. New York. Several pictures.

Harmon Foundation. 1935. *Negro Artists: An Illustrated Review of their Achievements*. New York.

Harrington, Oliver. 1958. *Boatsie and Others*. New York: Dodd, Mead. 100 cartoons.

H.B.L. 1926. Negro's Art Lives in His Wrought Iron. *New York Times Magazine*, August 8.

Hollingsworth, Alvin. 1957. Harlem (Drawings). *High*, December.

Howard University Bulletin. 1957. (March). *Art at the University*.

Janis, Sidney. 1942. *They Taught Themselves*, New York: The Dial Press. Includes Horace Pippin, Flora Lewis and Cleo Crawford.

Jewell, Edward Alden, 1928. A Negro Artist Plumbs the Negro Soul. *New York Times Magazine*, March 25. On Archibald Motley.

Johnson, James Weldon. 1927. *God's Trombones*. New York: Viking Press. Illustrated by Aaron Douglas.

Jones, Lois Mailou. 1952. *Peintures 1937–1951*. Tourcoing (France): Presses Georges Frère.

Junier, Allan (ed.). 1959. *Newsletter of the National Conference of Negro Artists*. November. For copies, or information, address Allan G. Junier, Box 33, Veterans Administration Hospital, Tuskegee, Alabama.

Landy, Jacob. 1958. William H. Johnson: Expressionist Turned Primitive. *Journal American Assoc. of University Women*, March. Several pictures.

Larkin, Oliver, 1949. *Art and Life in America*, New York: Rinehart. Quotations from pp. 29, 279.

Locke, Alain. 1936. *Negro Art: Past and Present*. Washington, D.C.: Associates in Negro Folk Education.

Locke, Alain, 1939. Advance on the Art Front. *Opportunity*, May. Several pictures.

Locke, Alain. 1940. *The Negro in Art*. Washington, D.C.: Associates in Negro Folk Education.

Locke, Alain. 1953. The Negro in the Arts. See Dover, C.

Lockhart, Alice. 1955. Claude Clark. *Motive*, March. Illustrated.

Lowenfeld, Viktor, 1944. The Negro Art in America. *Design*, September.

MacChesney, Clara. 1913. A Poet Painter of Palestine. *International Studio*, July. Pictures include *The Resurrection of Lazarus*.

Martinsen, Dick. 1955. Folk Art of Texas. *Houston Chronicle Rotogravure Magazine*, March 6. John Biggers and his class. Pictures in colour.

Miller, Henry, 1947. The Amazing and Invariable Beauford Delaney. In *Remember To Remember*. New York: New Directions.

Miller, Inez. 1956. John Biggers. *Southern Artist* (Houston, Texas), 2(2):14–19. Several illustrations.

Murray, Freeman. 1916. *Emancipation and the Freed in American Sculpture*. Washington, D.C.: Published by the Author.

Negro in Chicago, 1779–1929, The. 1929. Chicago: Washington Intercollegiate Club. Includes several reproductions of works of art.

Pearson, Ralph. 1954. *The Modern Renaissance in American Art*. New York: Harper. Illustrated discussions of Jacob Lawrence and Eldzier Cortor.

Pinchbeck, R. B. 1926. *The Virginia Negro Artisan and Tradesman*. Richmond: William Byrd's Press.

Pleasants, J. Hall. 1942. Joshua Johnston, The First American Negro Portrait Painter. *Maryland Historical Magazine* 37(2):121–149.

Porter, James. 1935. Malvin Gray Johnson. *Opportunity* (New York), April.

Porter, James. 1936. Versatile Interests of the Early Negro Artist. *Art in America and Elsewhere*, January.

Porter, James. 1943. *Modern Negro Art*. New York: Dryden. Quotations from pp. 23, 28, 171.

Porter, James, 1951. Robert S. Duncanson: Midwestern Romantic-Realist. *Art in America* 39(3): 99–154. Contains reproductions of 27 pictures by Duncanson.

Porter, James, 1955. The New Negro and Modern Art. See Logan, Rayford.

Porter, James. 1958. The Transcultural Affinities of African Negro Art. See Davis, John.

Reddick, L. D. 1954. Walter Simon: The Socialization of an American Negro Artist. *Phylon* (Atlanta University), 373–392.

Rodman, Selden. 1947. *Horace Pippin: A Negro Painter in America*. New York: Quadrangle Press.

Rodman, Selden. 1957. *Conversations with Artists*. New York: Devin-Adair. Includes Jacob Lawrence.

Rutledge, Anna Wells. 1949. Ned, a Negro Woodcarver. *Transactions American Philosophical Society*, 39:144.

Simms, Carroll, Mack, Joseph and Biggers, John. 1957. *Man and the World of Science*. A proposed research project dealing with the integration of murals and sculpture with architecture for the new Science Building, Department of Art, Texas Southern University.

Smith, Lucy, 1927. Some American Painters in Paris. *American Magazine of Art*, March. Includes Tanner.

Sutton, Denys. 1948. *American Painting*. London: Avalon Press.

Tanner, Henry. 1909. The Story of the Artist's Life. *World's Work*, January, February.

USIS. 1956. *American Art and Art Education*. New York and London. A book list.

USIS. 1958. *Books on Art*. New York and London.

USIS. 1958. *Negroes Enter Main Stream of American Art*. An illustrated feature distributed 'for use by newspapers, magazines, and radio stations'.

Waring, Laura and Reyneau, Betsy. No date. *Portraits of Outstanding Americans of Negro Origin*. A portfolio. New York: Harmon Foundation.

Werlein, Mrs Phillip. 1925. *The Wrought Iron Railings of Le Vieux Carré*. New Orleans: Published by the Author.

Some Catalogues

(Listed because of their introductions, pictures or biographical information.)

Albany Institute of History and Art. 1945. *The Negro Artist Comes of Age*. Albany, New York. Intros. by John Davis Hatch and Alain Locke.

Alston, Charles. 1958. *Exhibition of Paintings, Sculpture, Drawings and Watercolors*. New York: John Heller Gallery.

Alston, Frank. 1948. *Exhibition of Paintings and Watercolors*. Washington, D.C.: The Barnett Aden Gallery.

Alston, Frank. 1948. *Paintings*. Washington, D.C.: Barnett Aden Gallery. Intro., reprinted from *La Revue Moderne*, July 1948, by R. Clermont.

American Negro Exposition, Chicago. 1940. *The Art of the American Negro (1851–1940)*. Arranged by Alonzo Aden. Intro. by Alain Locke. Extensively illustrated.

Anderson, Sherwood and Caldwell, Erskine. 1935. *An Art Commentary on Lynching*. New York: Newton Galleries.

Art Institute of Chicago. 1923, 1931. *Exhibition by Artists of Chicago and Vicinity*. Reproductions of Motley's *Grandmother* and *Blues*.

Atlanta University. 1942–60. *Annual Art Exhibitions by Negro Artists*.

Barnett Aden Gallery. 1953. *Eighteen Washington Artists*. Washington, D.C. Intros. by James Porter and Agnes DeLano.

Biggers, John, 1953. *Contribution of the Negro Woman to American Life and Education* (Mural). Houston, Texas: Y.W.C.A.

Burke, Selma. 1958. *Sculptures and Drawings*. New York: Avant-Garde Gallery.

Burroughs, Margaret. 1945. *Exhibition of Oils, Water Colors, Prints, Ceramics*. Chicago: South Side Community Art Center. Intro. by Rex Goreleigh.

Carnegie Institute. 1944, 1947. *Painting in the United States*. Pittsburgh.

Carnegie Institute. 1955. *Pittsburgh International Exhibition of Contemporary Painting*. Pittsburgh.

Catlett, Elizabeth. 1948. *The Negro Woman*. Washington, D.C.: Barnett Aden Gallery. Intro. by Gwendolyn Bennett.

Clark, Claude. No date. Three pictures in a leaflet by Ruthermore Galleries, San Francisco.

Crichlow, Ernest. 1960. *Paintings and Drawings*. New York: ACA Gallery. Intro. by Lena Horne.

Dempsey, Richard. 1959. *Recent Paintings*. Washington, D.C.: Franz Bader Gallery.

Dempsey, Richard. 1951. *Recent Haitian American Paintings*. Washington, D.C.: Barnett Aden Gallery. Intro. by E. Franklin Frazier.

Douglas, Aaron. 1948. *Exhibition of Paintings*. Nashville (Tenn.): Fisk University International Student Center.

Douglas, Aaron. 1950. *Exhibition of Paintings*. Oklahoma: Stiles Street Y.W.C.A.

Driskell, David. 1957. *Exhibition of Paintings*, Washington, D.C.: Barnett Aden Gallery. Intro. by James Porter.

Fisk University. 1949. *Catalogue of the Alfred Stieglitz Collection*. Nashville, Tenn.

Harmon Foundation. 1928. *Exhibition of Fine Arts by American Negro Artists*, New York.

Harmon Foundation. 1933. *Exhibition by Negro Artists*. New York.

Hooks, Earl. 1959. Items 18–20 (18 illustrated) in Fifth Biennial Ceramic Exhibition. Indianapolis: John Herron Art Museum.

Howard, Humbert. 1959. *Paintings*. Washington, D.C.: Howard Univ. Gallery of Art.

Howard University. 1957. *An Exhibition of Paintings, Prints and Drawings by the Faculty of the Department of Art*. Washington, D.C.: Howard University Gallery of Art.

Hunt, Richard. 1958. *Sculpture*. New York: The Alan Gallery. Ten illustrations.

Institute of Int. Education. 1957. *News Bulletin*, December. Sculpture by Carroll Simms illustrated on pp. 28–30.

Lawrence, Jacob. 1946. *The Life of John Brown*. Washington, D.C.: Barnett Aden Gallery.

Lee-Smith, Hughie. 1955. *Exhibition of Paintings*. Washington, D.C.: Howard University Gallery of Art. Intro. by E. P. Richardson.

Lee-Smith, Hughie. 1958. *Catalogue of Paintings*. Washington, D.C.: Howard University Gallery of Art. Intro. by James Porter.

Lewis, Norman, 1958. *Paintings*. Washington, D.C.: Barnett Aden Gallery. Intro. by James Herring.

Library of Congress. 1940. 75 *Years of Freedom*. Washington, D.C.: U.S. Government Printing Office. Motley's *Uncle Bob* in colour.

Middleton, Samuel. 1958. *Exhibition*. New York: Contemporary Arts.

Morgan, Norma. 1954. *Paintings*. New York: Pachita Crespi Gallery.

Phillips Memorial Gallery. 1946.

Three Negro Artists: Horace Pippin, Jacob Lawrence and Richmond Barthé. Washington, D.C.

Pierce, Delilah. 1959. *Exhibition of Paintings*. Washington, D.C.: Margaret Dickey Gallery of Art.

Pippin, Horace. 1940. *Catalogue of Exhibition*. Philadelphia: Carlen Galleries. Intro. by Albert Barnes.

Pippin, Horace. 1941. *Recent Paintings*. Philadelphia: Carlen Galleries. Intro. by Albert Barnes.

Porter, James. 1948. *Recent Paintings and Drawings*. Washington, D.C.: Barnett Aden Gallery. Intro. by Adelyn Breeskin.

Schweicher, Curt and Delloye, Charles. 1958. *Neues Aus Der Neuen Malerei*. Schloss Morsbroich: Städtisches Museum Leverkusen. Reproduction of Beauford DeLaney's *Composition Jaune*.

Smithsonian Institute. 1933. *Exhibition of Works by Negro Artists at the National Gallery of Art*. Washington, D.C.

Staten, Douglas. No date. *Exhibition of Paintings*. Chicago: Southside Community Art Center.

Waring, Laura Wheeler. 1949. *In Memoriam: An Exhibition of Paintings*. Washington, D.C.: Howard University Gallery of Art. Intros. by James Herring and James Porter. Five paintings illustrated.

Washington, James. No date. *Paintings and Sculpture by Spazzali and Washington*. San Francisco: Feingarten Galleries.

Wells, James Lesesne. 1932. *Exhibition of Block Prints*. New York City: Delphic Studios.

Wells, James Lesesne. 1950. *Paintings and Prints*. Washington, D.C.: Barnett Aden Gallery. Intro. by Jacob Kainen.

White, Charles. 1947. *Recent Paintings*. New York: ACA Gallery; Washington, D.C.: Barnett Aden Gallery. Intro. by Robert Gwathmey.

White, Charles. 1950. *Drawings and Prints*. New York: ACA Gallery. Intro. by Howard Fast.

White, Charles. 1953. *Recent Paintings*. New York: ACA Gallery. Intro. by Herman Baron.

White, Charles. 1958. *Drawings and Prints*. New York: ACA Gallery. Intro. by Harry Belafonte.

Wilson, Ellis. 1954. *Impressions of Haiti*. New York: Contemporary Arts.

Woodruff, Hale. 1956. The American Negro Artist. *Eight New York Painters*. Ann Arbor: University of Michigan.

Margaret Burroughes
Mexican Landscape

Courtesy
Marion Perkins

GROTESQUE JUG
EARLY NINETEENTH CENTURY
Courtesy The Index of American Design,
National Gallery of Art, Washington, D.C.

THE BACKGROUND

History offers no date for the beginnings of art by American Negroes, but the craft background goes back to the log cabin days of the New World colonies. Later, as wealth brought increasing luxury, chosen slaves were encouraged to supply the growing variety of needs in ways that added aesthetic satisfactions to utility. Some thereby found opportunities to pass into the rising group of free Negro artisans.

In fact, coloured labourers provided much more than the enormous manpower required for building and maintaining the great mansions of early America. Their chief craft products ranged from crude iron utensils to the famous wrought iron of New Orleans, from simple furniture to impressively carved woodwork, from earthen containers to uniquely designed and attractively glazed jars, from stable leathers to finely tooled bags and book covers, and from plain cottons to embroidered frocks and patterned textiles of delicate charm.

The transition from the crafts to the arts was promoted by prosperous coloured families to a much greater extent than is generally known. Their cultural rôle is suggested by Mr Clarence Laughlin's fascinating photographs of *Melrose*, the Metoyer home near Natchitoches, Louisiana, which began as an ex-slave's cabin, of astonishing distinction inside, about 1750. The Metoyers shared with others intent on tradition a noticeable fondness for portraits of themselves, but coloured and liberal white patronage offered no more than occasional orders for 'likenesses' to Negroes who maintained themselves in other ways— usually as sign painters and engravers to whom a portrait was only a variation of their everyday tasks. The history of American Negro painting starts, in the last quarter of the eighteenth century, with these limners.

Fortunate Negroes also built elegant homes with slave labour. The famous Melrose (originally Yucca) Plantation, Natchitoches, Louisiana, began as a cabin (*left*) erected about 1750 by Marie Thérèse, a freed slave who married Thomas Metoyer from Paris. It was built of earth, mixed with moss and deer hair, packed between cypress planks, but the interior acquired something of the grand manner (*below*). Augustine, Madame Metoyer's eldest son, is the subject of the large portrait (signed Feuville, 1829). He is pointing to St Augustine's Church which, as the leader of the mulatto community, he built for his people in 1829.

Photographs: *Courtesy Clarence John Laughlin*

Plate 2

Madame Metoyer owned fifty-eight slaves. Her 'African House' (*right*), now unique in the United States, was built of brick and cypress about the time of her own home and is almost as impressive externally. One of the two rooms of the ground floor was used as a store; the other as a prison for slaves who wanted more than Madame would give.

The central part of the main building (*below*) of Melrose Plantation was built by her grandson, Louis Metoyer, in 1833, but racialism was already submerging the mulattoes—and in 1847 the Plantation passed to the whites.

Photographs: *Courtesy Clarence John Laughlin*

Plate 3

Plate 4

The Metoyer family portraits are among the earliest surviving paintings of American Negroes—Franco-African and other mulattoes of the United States are now Negroes in the American sense. One of Marie Metoyer's grandsons, possibly Louis, is the subject of the portrait (*left*); the painting (*above left*) is of her granddaughter. Both are unsigned and undated, but are probably the work of a mulatto painter before 1830.

The Metoyers were evidently home builders of discrimination—and American artists and artisans prospered as the needs of such families increased. Ornamentation flourished, but remained controlled by good taste for many decades. The Franklin stove (*above*), in the main bedroom of Melrose Plantation, is an example. It was made in the Philadelphia foundries before Louisiana became an American state.

Photographs: *Courtesy Clarence John Laughlin*

Plate 5

Art begins with crafts—and the craftsmen who supplied the domestic needs of early America were mostly slaves. Here, by courtesy of The Index of American Design, National Gallery of Art, Washington, D.C., are some examples of their work.

Above: Wrought iron latch, New Orleans. Blue silk dress, Assumption Parish, Louisiana. *Below:* Clock, 1833, stained cypress body, St James' Parish, Louisiana. Preserving jar, 1859, glazed light olive with burnt sienna, dull rose and light blue markings, by Dave & Baddler, Louis Miles Pottery, Aiken County, S. Carolina. Grotesque jug, grey stoneware glazed olive green, of a common 'slave pottery' type.

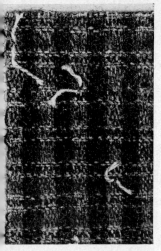

Above: Tooled leather keybag, 1858, made in plantation tannery, Buckingham County, Virginia. *Left:* Wool-filled comforter (fragment), 1835, of domestic wool, Bowling Green, Kentucky. *Below:* Brass servants' bell, 1815, Natchez, Mississippi.

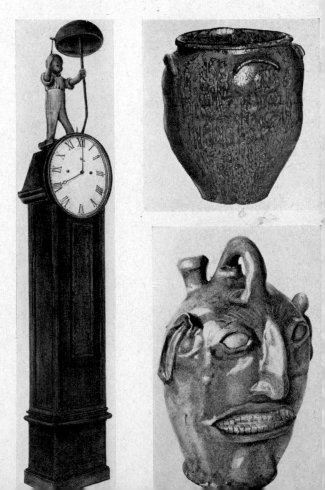

Woodcarving was also an 'ancestral art' of the slaves in America, but it could not survive in the circumstances imposed on them. An exception is the *Hardwood Stick (right)*, 1863, by Henry Gudgell of Missouri. Its spirally carved handle and motifs relate it to West African carvings. The *Hen (right)*, made of fitted pieces of cypress, also suggests African influence. It is attributed to a slave of the pirate Jean La Fitte, Louisiana.

Courtesy of the Index of American Design; and the Art Institute of Chicago for Preacher.

Early American personalities made little impression on Negroes, but the *Walnut Doll* below, hollowed for fixing to a post, shows some resemblance to George Washington. New hopes brought new stimuli—and in the painted carving of the *Negro Preacher* we feel the power of primitive American Negro sculpture.

Plate 6

Family portraits are indispensable to home builders—and in early America many interesting limners, or self-taught portrait painters, supplied their needs. *Joshua Johnston* was one of the earliest. His stiff two-dimensional, typically 'primitive' portraits were popular with the aristocrats of Baltimore between 1789 and 1825.

Right: Mrs John Moale and Her Granddaughter Ellin North Moale (c. 1800). 40½ × 35⅛.
Courtesy of the owner Roswell P. Russell, Baltimore, and the Frick Art Reference Library, New York City.

Below: The James McCormick Family (c. 1804). 50 × 70.
Courtesy of the Maryland Historical Society, Baltimore

Plate 7

William Simpson   OIL
Jermain Loguen   1835

Plate 8

Patrick Reason   ENGRAVING
Granville Sharp   1835

Above: Courtesy of Howard University's Gallery of Art, Washington, D.C., and James Porter, whose book (Modern Negro Art, New York 1943) suggested their inclusion.

G. W. Hobbs   PASTEL
Richard Allen   1785

Joshua Johnston's position as the first Negro limner needs to be definitively challenged. Many other Negro portraitists, some of whom had overcome his limitations, were known in his day—and before it. In Baltimore itself, Richard Allen, who later became the first Bishop of the African Methodist Episcopal Church, had his portrait painted in 1785 by a friend who was almost certainly the Rev. G. W. Hobbs. In colonial Louisiana, as the Metoyer portraits suggest, there were good mulatto painters, among whom Julien Hudson of New Orleans is known by name. In New York, Patrick Reason achieved a reputation as an engraver; in Boston, William Simpson's forceful portraits brought him numerous clients.

Julien Hudson
*Colonel Jean
Michel Fortier Jr.*
OIL   *c.* 1830

Courtesy of the Louisiana State Museum by arrangement with Ernest C. Wagner, Dillard University, New Orleans. Photo: Hubert A. Giles, Dillard University

Leslie Bolling
Washerwoman
KNIFE CARVING 1933
Courtesy the Harmon
Foundation, New York

RECENT PRIMITIVES

The limners represented in the previous plates are among the Negro forerunners of a lively American folk art from before Edward Hicks (1780–1849) to Grandma Moses (born 1860). In it, as Alice Ford has said, there are 'the memories of Everyman . . . his favourite scenes and legends . . . his fantasy . . . his face, fields and lore . . . his heart, his history'. It is a native art—naïve, sincere and charged with good will—free from schools, mannerisms and imported influences.

The Depression quickened its appreciation, for cultural patriotism is a natural response to times of stress; and several institutions gave content to awareness by a series of exhibitions beginning in 1930 with 'American Primitives' at the Newark Museum, New Jersey, and 'American Folk Art 1750–1900' at the Museum of Modern Art, New York. In London, a selection from the whole range of 'American Primitive Art 1670–1954' was shown at the Whitechapel Art Gallery in 1955.

Horace Pippin was a major discovery of the 'thirties. It is not true that he was 'the first important Negro painter to appear on the American scene', but his vision, sensitiveness, social consciousness, precision, dramatic power and exuberant use of colour certainly put him in the company of the leading American 'primitives'. No equally exciting self-taught Negro artist has succeeded him, though John Robinson deserves wide acclaim. Alfred Barr has stated that he does 'not know a finer landscape than Joseph Pickett's *Manchester Valley*', but is there a 'primitive' who has excelled Robinson's *Anacostia Hills*?

We have included in this section an example, William Johnson's *Jesus and the Three Marys*, of the influence of the primitive manner on an academically trained painter. Others, notably Irene Clark's *A Mansion on Prairie Avenue*, will be found elsewhere in this book.

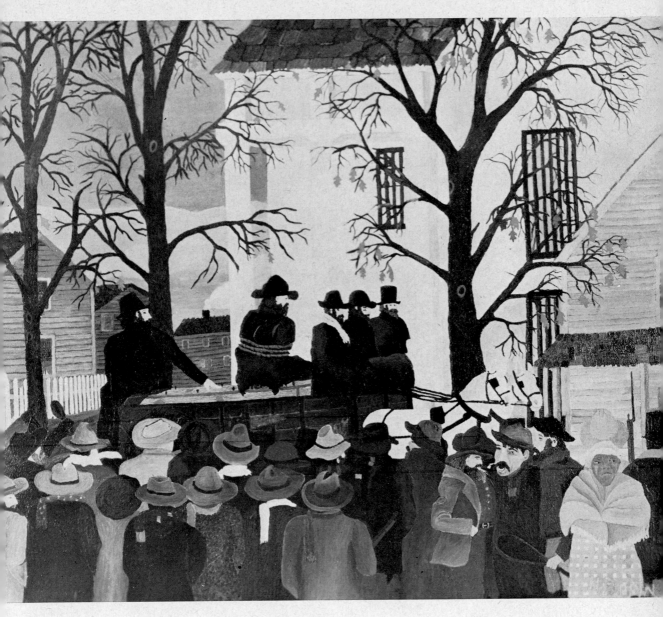

Plate 9
Horace Pippin
John Brown Goes to His Hanging
OIL   1942

Horace Pippin

The Den
OIL   1945
*Courtesy Robert Carlen,
Carlen Galleries,
Philadelphia, and the
owners, Mr and Mrs
Arnold Gingrich, New York*

Plate 10

Cabin in the Cotton
OIL   1944
*Courtesy Mr and Mrs
Roy R. Neuberger, New
York, and the Carnegie
Institute, Pittsburgh*

Plate 11

William Johnson
Jesus and the Three Marys
Courtesy Barnett Aden Gallery,
Washington, D.C.

Cleo Crawford
Christmas
OIL   1937

Courtesy Sidney Janis from his book
They Taught Themselves
(The Dial Press, New York, 1942)

John Robinson
My Grandparents

Anacostia Hills
OIL   1944
*Howard University's
Gallery of Art,
Washington, D.C.*

Plate 12

Photographs: *Courtesy
Barnett Aden Gallery,
Washington, D.C.*

John Robinson
Outdoor Art Fair
OIL   1946
Courtesy Barnett Aden
Gallery, Washington, D.C.

Plate 13

Thomas Jefferson Flanagan
Fishing on the Quarters
OIL   1957
Courtesy Atlanta University,
Atlanta, Georgia

Jewel Simon
The Outing
WATERCOLOUR

Plate 14

Frank Rawlings
Attacked
PAINTS AND WATERCOLOUR PENCILS
Courtesy the Artist

Plate 15

James Washington

Above: *Nesting Bird*
GRANITE AND WOOD 1957
*Courtesy Mrs Robert Block,
Seattle, Washington*

Top right: *Mexican Market*
OIL   1957
Courtesy the Artist

Right: *Sitting Bird*
GRANITE AND WOOD   1956
*Courtesy Mrs Charles Frick,
Seattle, Washington*

Leslie Bolling
Salome
KNIFE CARVING 1934
*Courtesy Harmon
Foundation, New York*

Plate 16

William Edmonson
Preacher
LIMESTONE 1938
*Courtesy R. Lynn Baker,
New York, and (photograph)
the Museum of Modern Art,
New York*

Daniel Warburg
*The Holcombe Memorial, New Orleans
Courtesy A. Weiblen Works, Ernest C.
Wagner and Hubert A. Giles, New Orleans*

Both Edmonson and Warburg were gravestone cutters.
Warburg, a nephew of Eugene Warburg, was a master
craftsman who died 'undiscovered'. Edmonson, luckier in
his period, became a sensation as a vigorous primitive.

Patrick Reason
De Witt Clinton
PENCIL AND WASH 1835
*Courtesy Howard University,
Washington, D.C.,
and James Porter*

THE NINETEENTH CENTURY

The main achievement of 'atelier art' by American Negroes in the nineteenth century was the proof that they could make art according to the standards and sentimentalities of their day. They paid homage to anti-slavery and other sponsors, but failed, understandably, to contribute significantly to the progress of their own people or to the advancement of American art.

Edward Bannister was a partial exception. Urged by a deeply rooted love of woods and waters, and an idealistic view of life, he was the first Negro to earn recognition as a truly native American landscape painter. He is remembered, too, as one of the founding members of the famous Providence Art Club.

Robert Duncanson, the first Negro genre painter of consequence, is more typical of the period. A Romantic, much influenced by Scott and Tennyson, he missed the great days of Romanticism, while his affinities with the Hudson River School lacked the benefit of association. Sometimes descending to the level of the moralizing family weeklies popular in his day, his landscapes often have a compelling charm, while his portraits are usually worthy of the striking personalities who engaged his attention.

The first Negro sculptor, Eugene Warbourg, who lived mostly in Europe, was also a Romantic aloof from the Negro scene—so aloof that his importance has been completely obscured by Edmonia Lewis, his junior by twenty years.

With greater good fortune in his masters, Henry Tanner achieved a reputation unequalled by any other Negro artist before the First World War. His *Banjo Player* is a token of what he could have done for his community and for American art, but he preferred to live in Paris and to find his subjects in the Bible and the Holy Land. Forgotten in France, his name survives in America by the circumstance of birth and the perpetuating will of historically minded Negroes.

Plate 17

Robert Duncanson (1817–72)
Blue Hole, Little Miami River
OIL: $42\frac{1}{4} \times 29\frac{1}{4}$ 1851
Courtesy Cincinnati Art Museum

Nicholas Langworth
OIL   1858
Courtesy Ohio Mechanics
Institute, Cincinnati, and
(photo) Clarence Koehn

Plate 18

Robert Duncanson

Uncle Tom and Little Eva
OIL   1853
Courtesy Detroit Institute of Arts

The Drunkard's Plight
OIL   1845
Detroit Institute of Arts

Edmonia Lewis (1845–c. 1890)
Charles Sumner
PLASTER   1876
Wilberforce University, Ohio

Eugene Warbourg (1825–1861)
John Young Mason
MARBLE   c. 1853
Virginia Historical Society, Richmond

Plate 19

May Howard Jackson (1877–1931)
Dean Kelly Miller
PLASTER   1914
Howard University, Washington, D.C.

Meta Warrick Fuller (1877–?)
Water Boy
Courtesy Harmon Foundation

Edward Bannister (1828–1901)

Sabin Point, Narragansett Bay
OIL   *c. 1875*
*Courtesy Brown University,
Providence, Rhode Island*

Sad Memories
PENCIL   1882
*Courtesy William Alden
Brown, Providence, R.I.*

Plate 20

Photographs: *Courtesy
Photographic Laboratory,
Brown University,
Providence, R.I.*

Edward Bannister
After the Storm
OIL   1875
*Courtesy Museum of the Rhode Island
School of Design, Providence, R.I.*
Photograph: *Courtesy James Porter from
his book* Modern Negro Art.

Plate 21

Flower Study
Courtesy Providence Art Club
Photograph: *Photographic Laboratory,
Brown University, Providence, R.I.*

Plate 22

Henry Tanner (1859–1937)

The Wailing Wall, Jerusalem
OIL   1915
*Courtesy Philadelphia Academy
of the Fine Arts, Philadelphia*

Plate 23 ▶

The Banjo Lesson
OIL   1890
*Hampton Institute,
Hampton, Virginia*

Annunciation
OIL   1898
*Courtesy Philadelphia
Museum of Art
(Wilstach Collection)*

Henry Tanner
Christ and Nicodemus
OIL   1900
*Courtesy Pennsylvania
Academy of the Fine
Arts, Philadelphia*

Plate 24

William Harper (1873–1910)
Landscape
OIL   1906
Courtesy Joseph A. Kersey

Phillip Hampton
Cartoon for a Mural
Courtesy the Artist

THE MURALISTS

Rivera, Orozco and their colleagues held that monumental and episodic art should be public property inspired by the people and created by officially sponsored artists. This approach was sufficiently unpopular in the United States to secure the destruction of Rivera's *Man at the Crossroads* in the Rockefeller Centre, but it stimulated many American artists who also benefited from Government support during the great days of the Roosevelt Era.

Few mastered the technological problems, but many produced interesting murals and some still do so. Except for the highly symbolic geometrical suggestiveness of Aaron Douglas, most of the Negro muralists were influenced by what can be called the Rivera manner, for it was admirably suited to their intention to dramatize the epic struggles and successes of their people. Unfortunately, the manner was so suitable that it confined originality, while the themes were sometimes too complex and intrinsically dramatic for pictorial narration without great gifts for selectiveness and design.

Nevertheless, some transcended imitation and mere recording (important enough in any community needing the values and motivations that come from looking at its history) by sheer intensity, understanding, draughtsmanship and feeling for design. Among them Hale Woodruff is the pioneer and still the leader, though his brilliantly executed murals leave the uncomfortable impression that they only represent carefully chosen subjects. They do not communicate the depth of purpose which distinguishes Charles White's *Contribution of the Negro to American Democracy*—a purpose so passionate that even his sketches for it are finished works. We show one opposite.

Plate 26

Charles White
The Contribution of the
Negro to American Democracy

Hampton Institute, Hampton,
Virginia, 1943.
Courtesy J. J. Brady

Aaron Douglas
Drama   1934
A panel in the
Library of Fisk University,
Nashville, Tennessee.
Courtesy of the Librarian,
Arna Bontemps

Plate 27

Charles Alston   *Magic and Medicine*
Sketch for a panel in the Harlem Hospital, New York,
commissioned by the W.P.A. Federal Art Project, 1937.
Courtesy the General Services Administration,
National Archives and Records Service, Washington, D.C.

Plate 28

Hale Woodruff
*The Amistad Murals in
the Savery Library of
Talladega College,
Talladega, Alabama*, 1939

Panel One. *The Mutiny
Aboard the Amistad*, 1839

Panel Two. *The Amistad Slaves on
Trial at New Haven, Connecticut*, 1840

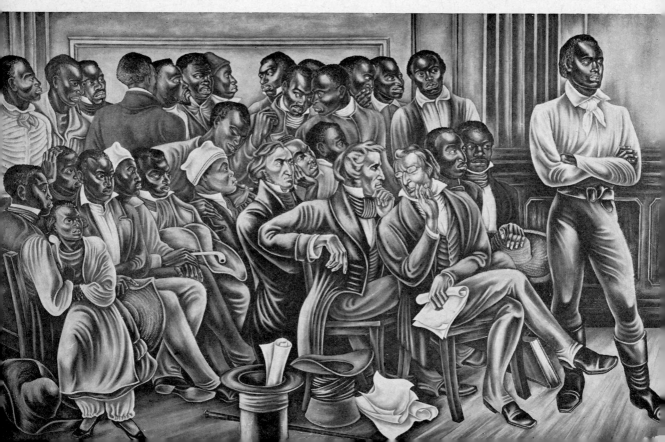

Panel Three. *The Return
to Africa*, 1842

Archibald Motley
United States Mail
Panel, 1936, in the Post
Office at Wood River, Illinois
*Courtesy the General Services
Administration, National
Archives and Records Service,
Washington, D.C.*

Plate 30

Elmer Brown
Freedom of Expression
Mural on masonite, 1942
Men's City Club, Cleveland, Ohio
Courtesy the Artist

HE CONTRIBUTION OF NEGRO WOMAN TO
DONATED BY REV. FRED T. LEE
IN MEMORY OF HIS WIFE
MRS. DELA LEE
AMERICAN LIFE AND EDUCATION
HARRIET TUBMAN LED 400 SLAVES IN ESCAPE FROM BONDAGE

John Biggers

The Contribution of Negro Women to American Life and Education 1953

Donated by the Rev. Fred T. Lee to the Y.W.C.A., Houston, Texas

Plate 31

Slave
Detail from the mural shown above

Allan Crite
City of God
Altar painting in St.
Augustine's, Brooklyn, N.Y.
Courtesy the Artist

Plate 32

Richmond Barthé
Exodus
Dance
MARBLE RELIEFS 1938
Harlem River
Houses, N.Y.C.
*Courtesy General
Services Administration,
National Archives and
Records Service,
Washington, D.C.*

THE NEGRO PERSONALITY

Among the amiabilities of Empire building, America inherited a tradition of portrait painting which grew, with such
masters as Thomas Eakins (1848–1916),
into a proud record of character and purpose. The Negro contribution to it began
with the self-taught artists, but before 1920
it did not go beyond the notably competent
documentation of the Negro personality by
Edward Harleston, Laura Wheeler Waring
and John Hardrick. The occasional portraits of other Negro artists, and almost all
Negro artists seem unusually capable of
painting a good portrait whatever their
creative interests, were often up to their
standards. White sympathizers, such as
Betsy Graves Reyneau, whose portraits of
Alain Locke and *Charles Johnson* are reproduced at the beginning of this book, often
equalled, and sometimes excelled, these
pictures.

Archibald Motley's portraits took competence into distinction. His achievement
will be complete when his unity of technique
with compassion and group consciousness
is surpassed, but at present his rivals include
no peers. Among them Aaron Douglas and
James Porter (whose early *Sarah*, unfortunately destroyed by fire, is one of the
most haunting portraits in all Negro
painting) lead the older, and John Wilson
and James Reed the younger, generation
of realistic portrait painters. Charles White
is, of course, more than worthy of the
Motley standard, but he does not work in
oils.

Regrettably, for an artist's view of himself is always interesting, we have had no
space for a representative selection of the
many outstanding self-portraits by Negro
artists. Fred Flemister in the rôle of an old
master, *Man with Brush*, remains one of
the most forceful after twenty years.

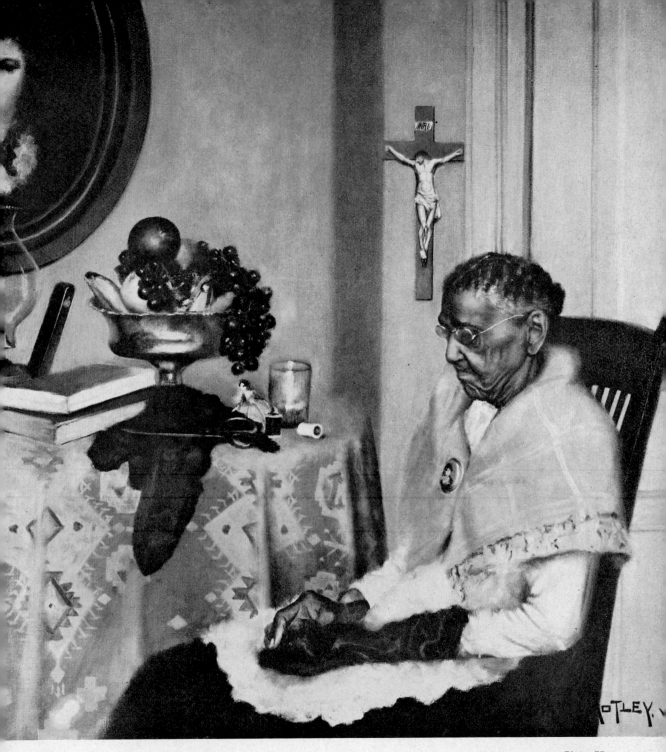

Plate 33
Archibald Motley
Mending Socks
OIL   1923
*Courtesy Art Institute
of Chicago*

Archibald Motley
Old Snuff Dipper
OIL   1928

John Hardrick
Aunty
OIL   1933

Plate 34

Edwin Harleston (1882–1931)
The Old Servant
OIL   1928

Malvin Johnson (1896–1934)
Meditation
OIL   *c.* 1932

Photos: James Latimer Allen
Courtesy Harmon Foundation

Alonzo Aden 1947

Plate 35

Laura Waring (1887–1948)

W. E. Burghardt Du Bois
1945

Courtesy Harmon Foundation

James Weldon Johnson
1945

Mother and Daughter
c. 1925

James Porter
Sarah
OIL 1928

Courtesy Harmon Foundation

Plate 36

Dorothy Porter
OIL 1948
Courtesy the Artist

Rex Goreleigh
The Twins
OIL 1958
Courtesy the Artist

Charles White
Fred O'Neal, Rex Ingram
and Georgia Burke in
'Anna Lucasta'
WOLFF CRAYON   1958
Courtesy the Artist

Plate 37

Fred Flemister
Man with Brush
OIL   1940
Courtesy Barnett Aden Gallery,
Washington, D.C.

Plate 38

James Reed
Depressed
OIL   1950
Courtesy Atlanta University
Art Exhibition, Atlanta, Ga

Lois Mailou Jones
Jennie
OIL   1943
Courtesy Department of Arts and
Sciences, International Business
Machines Corporation, New York

Ernest Crichlow
Lend Me a Hand (detail)
*Courtesy American Society
of African Culture, New York*

Hale Woodruff
Countee Cullen
OIL   *c.* 1926
*Courtesy Ida Cullen
Cooper, New York*

Plate 39

Ernest Crichlow
The Domestic
*Courtesy American Society
of African Culture, New York*

John Wilson
My Brother
OIL   1942
Courtesy the Artist

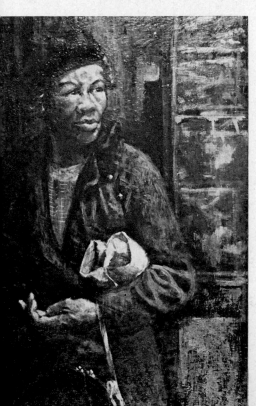

Eldzier Cortor
Skin Deep
OIL   1947
Courtesy the Artist

Kitty Chavis
Untitled
OIL 1959
Courtesy Creative Artists Guild, New York

Plate 40

Charles Sebree
Head of Woman
GOUACHE *c.* 1940
Courtesy Barnett Aden Gallery

THE FEEL OF AMERICA

111

America, as Langston Hughes has said in a stirring poem, 'never was America' to its Negro people, but 'its dream lies deep in the heart of me'. So deep that to James Weldon Johnson the tragedy of crossing over into the 'unknown dark' was that he would never again know the 'subtle spells' of his city, never again pulse to 'Manhattan's sights and sounds, her smells, her crowds, her throbbing force, the thrill that comes from being of her a part. . . .'

American Negro artists have accordingly responded to their native land—and it is their native land—with a feeling, whatever their manner and awareness of beauty or ugliness, we can share in these plates and elsewhere in this book. John Wilson turns from social protest to loving pictures of his own Roxbury, Massachusetts; Allan Freelon brings us the regional poetry of Gloucester, Massachusetts, as William Vaughan Moody knew it:

A mile behind is Gloucester town
Where the fishing fleet puts in,
A mile ahead the land dips down
And the woods and farms begin.
Here, where the moors stretch free
In the high blue afternoon,
Are the marching sun and talking sea. . . .
Scattering wide or blown in ranks,
Yellow and white or brown,
Boats and boats from the fishing banks
Come home to Gloucester town. . . .

Moreover, in their different and 'more contemporary' ways, Hughie Lee-Smith's uniquely expressed comments on the loneliness and frustration of city life, the compelling charm with which Stan Williamson invites us to old Chicago, the grim reminders of larger truths by Edward Loper and John Howard, and the abstractions of urban scenes by Richard Dempsey, Delilah Pierce and Mildred Thompson, suggest that Negro sensitiveness to the feel of America is creating developments in art that are 'new', interesting—and American.

Plate 41 ▶

John Wilson
Roxbury Landscape
Courtesy Atlanta
University, Georgia

112

Allan Freelon

*Gloucester Harbour,
Mass.*
OIL   1930
*Collection: Miss
Caroline Slotter*

Plate 42
Photos: *Courtesy
the Artist*

*Sand Dunes,
E. Gloucester*
OIL   1930
*Collection: Mrs
Constance Taylor*

Marvin Smith
Greenwood Lake
OIL   1939
Collection: Judge
Hubert Delaney,
New York City
Courtesy Barnett
Aden Gallery,
Washington, D.C.

Plate 43

Rex Goreleigh
House on Canal
Road
OIL   1958
Courtesy the Artist

Edward Loper
Quarry

Dox Thrash
Rugged Homes
CARBORUNDUM PRINT

Plate 44

Frank Moore
Street Corner
Courtesy Creative
Artists Guild

Walter Simon
Apartment on Washington Street
Courtesy the Artist

Stan Williamson

Houses in Chieago
1959

Plate 45

Courtesy the Artist

Old Dwellings 1958
OIL AND CASEIN

Leedell Moorehead
Across the Tracks
CASEIN   1959

Lewis Stephens
Country
WATERCOLOUR   1956

John Howard
Arkansas Landscape
1950

Plate 46

Photos: *Courtesy*
Atlanta University
Art Exhibition

Hughie Lee-Smith
Impedimenta
OIL   1958
Coll: Parish Museum,
Southampton, Long I.
*Courtesy Janet Nessler
Gallery, New York*

Plate 47

Richard Dempsey
Cityscape
OIL   1958
Courtesy the Artist

Mildred Thompson
Coney Island
OIL   1958
Courtesy the Artist

Plate 48

Delilah Pierce
Waterfront
OIL   1958
*Courtesy Barnett
Aden Gallery,
Washington, D.C.*

Hale Woodruff
Returning Home
BLOCK PRINT 1939
Courtesy Harold
Benjamin, London

THE NEGRO SCENE

The American Negro scene has seldom included the idyllic though ragged paradise of Eastman Johnson's *Old Kentucky Home*, but we see little of its realities in the presentation of American art: among the 290 paintings in the 'continuous and all-embracing' exhibition on 'Life in America' at the Metropolitan Museum of Art, New York, 1939, Negro life was confined to eight pre-Abolition pictures more or less touching on it.

Some early white artists did, of course, concern themselves affectionately, and not always sentimentally, with Negroes; and in recent years more than a few have interpreted the Negro scene forcefully. But there remains a difference between sympathetic looking at and intimate looking in—the kind of difference that separates the intention and content, though their manner and subjects are similar, of the Harlem scenes of Miguel Covarrubias and the equally stark commentaries of Archibald Motley.

So it is fortunate that a large number of Negro artists have revealed the everyday living, the rich personalities, the joys and sorrows, the courage, faith and successes, of their own people. This is their greatest achievement and, while there is a separate Negro minority in America, it will remain their proper function to enlarge it. Their purpose should not limit their style, their interests beyond their group, or their search for universals. Indeed, they might discover that all the universals can be found within their own people and creatively transformed.

The following pictures, and many others in this book, are a small token of their efforts. They concern the lives and progress of one-tenth of a nation ignored by the exhibition on 'Life in America' and allowed to claim attention in Emily Davie's quasi-official *Profile of America* (1954), in which 'America speaks for itself', through the lone voice of Booker T. Washington. This situation is changing—and the Negroness of Negro artists will undoubtedly improve it further.

Plate 49
Irene Clark
A Mansion on Prairie Avenue
Courtesy the Artist

Malvin Johnson
Thinnin' Corn
OIL   1934
Photo: *Courtesy Barnett*
Aden Gallery, Washington, D.C.

Hale Woodruff
The Teamster's Place
WATER COLOUR 1934
Courtesy Harmon
Foundation, New York

Phillip Hampton
Young Girls of Savannah
GOUACHE   1954
Courtesy the Artist

Plate 50

George Neal
The Red House
Courtesy Thelma
Kirkpatrick

Fred Flemister
The Mourners
Courtesy Atlanta
University

Plate 51

William Walker
Faith
1958

John Wilson
Incident
CONTE CRAYON 1952

Plate 52

Eldzier Cortor
Americana
OIL   1947
*Courtesy Carnegie
Institute, Pittsburgh*

Archibald Motley

Stomp
OIL   1927

Gettin' Religion
OIL   1948
*Courtesy Art Institute
of Chicago*

Chicken Shack
OIL   1936
*Courtesy General Services
Administration, National
Archives and Records Service,
Washington, D.C.*

Plate 53
Allan Crite
Tyre Jumping
OIL   1936

Charles Davis
Perhaps Tomorrow
Courtesy Barnett
Aden Gallery

Plate 54

Charles White
Mother and Child
WOLFF CRAYON   1953
Courtesy Mrs Frances White

Harper Phillips
Lullabye
OIL   1957

Charles Alston
Family
OIL   1955
Courtesy Whitney Museum
of American Art, New York

Hughie Lee-Smith
Boy with Tyre
OIL   1955
*Courtesy Detroit
Institute of Arts*

Jacob Lawrence
*In the evening
evangelists preach and
sing on the street corners*
GOUACHE 1943
*Courtesy Mr and Mrs Roy
R. Neuberger, New York*

Plate 55

Eldzier Cortor
Loneliness
OIL   1940
Courtesy Barnett Aden Gallery

Aaron Douglas
*The Memorial Chapel
Fisk University*
WATER COLOUR   1958
Courtesy the Artist

Plate 56

John Wilson
Mother and Child
OIL   1943
*Courtesy Carnegie
Institute, Pittsburg*

William Johnson
Flowers to the Teacher
OIL   *c.* 1940
Courtesy Barnett Aden Gallery

Richard Dempsey
Dr Charles Richard Drew
OIL   1946
*Courtesy Department of Arts
and Sciences, I.B.M.*

Elton Fax
Dr Seth Cudjoe of Ghana
Courtesy the Artist

THE NEGRO PAINTER ABROAD

'It is axiomatic', James Weldon Johnson has rightly said, 'that the artist achieves his best when working at his best with the material he knows best. And it goes without saying that the material which the Negro knows best comes out of the life and experience of the coloured people in America.' Therefore, the works of American Negro artists outside America are seldom more than exercises important to their own development, but where they go, and what they do when they get there, is interesting, especially if their responses have the quality of an almost native feeling.

On the whole, Negro creative workers have neglected Africa, though the ties of far away kinship, and the opportunities for mannerisms afforded by the 'ancestral arts', have been appealing. Recently, however, the rise of African nationalisms has compelled their attention and will do so increasingly and perhaps productively. Meanwhile, there is only some visual reportage, such as the accomplished drawings of Elton Fax or the water colours of Aaron Douglas.

Haiti has long been irresistible to Negro artists, largely because it is an Africa away from Africa. Ellis Wilson is a regular visitor whose colourful impressions have the vitality of native folkart.

France has warmed so many Negro artists that a pleasing book could easily be filled with what they saw and felt. It would show more emphatically than we can here that the vision and palette of Lois Mailou Jones, who is very proudly a Negro artist at home, are lovingly French.

William Johnson, with the advantage of long residence, equalled her achievement in Denmark; and others have been comparably successful elsewhere—James Porter in Cuba, for instance. Britain, reputedly as chilly spiritually as it is climatically, has also known itinerant Negro artists. Norma Morgan has even been overcome by the fays and bogles of its moorlands and rocks.

Plate 57 ▶

Ellis Wilson
Bird Vendor
OIL   1953
*Courtesy Contemporary
Arts Inc., New York*

132

James Porter
Haitian Market Women
OIL   1947
*Courtesy Jacques Antione
and the Artist*

Ellis Wilson

Paysannes
OIL   1954
*Courtesy Contemporary
Arts Inc., New York*

Plate 58

St. Marc, Haiti
OIL   1954
Courtesy the Artist

Plate 59
Richard Dempsey
View from my Room, Haiti
OIL   1957
Courtesy the Artist

Rain
OIL 1950

Claude Clark

Primitive Mill
OIL 1950
*Courtesy Harmon
Foundation, N.Y.C.*

Plate 60

*Courtesy Ruthermore
Galleries, San Francisco*

Sponge Fisherman
OIL 1950

Plate 61
Lois Mailou Jones
Speracedes, France

Archibald Motley
*The Jockey Club,
Paris*
OIL   1929
*Courtesy Harmon
Foundation, New York*

Plate 62

Lois Mailou Jones
*Coin de la Rue
Médard, Paris*
OIL   1947
*Courtesy the Phillips
Gallery, Washington*

William Johnson
Kerteminde Harbour, Denmark
Courtesy Harmon Foundation

Plate 63

Palmer Hayden
St Servan, France
Courtesy Harmon Foundation

James Porter
Cuban Bus
OIL 1946
Courtesy Howard University

James Wells
Interlude
OIL   1949
Courtesy the Artist

Aaron Douglas

Street Scene, Accra

Tower Bridge, London
WATERCOLOURS 1956
Courtesy the Artist

Norma Morgan
Badenoch, Inverness
OIL   1958
Courtesy the Artist

Earl Hooks
Louis Armstrong
CLAY PLAQUE 1958
Courtesy the Artist

SCULPTURE AND CERAMICS

According to Vasari 'All the most celebrated sculptors since Masaccio's day have become excellent and industrious by studying their art' through close attention to Masaccio's frescoes in the chapel of Santa Maria del Carmine at Florence. Few Negro sculptors can have sat before them, like Henry Moore, with a sketchbook, nor is their work really monumental, except for Robert Crump's rather ordinary statue of Leonidas Merritt on Minnesota's Iron Mountain and Richmond Barthé's heroic figures of Toussaint L'Ouverture and Dessalines at Port-au-Prince, Haiti; but the impact of much Negro sculpture is that of comparable strength, simplicity and 'immensity of life'.

Barthé's sculpture is invariably charged with this immensity: all Negro history, potentiality and hope broods in *The Negro Looks Ahead*. It is a quiet piece, quietly executed; in others we feel at once his profound concern with what Rodin called 'the latent heroism of natural movement'. Thus, it is not surprising that, with Sargent Johnson, whose manner is more sophisticated and stylized, he raised the long tradition of American Negro sculpture to new levels in the 'twenties and 'thirties. Today, though he lives in Jamaica and is busy with painting, he still promotes that tradition.

The same gift for communicating immensity distinguishes the carving and moulding of many other Negro sculptors —Elizabeth Catlett, William Artis, Ed Wilson, Marion Perkins and Henry Bannarn are among those who are inspired by social awareness. There is immensity, too, in the metal constructions of Barbara Chase and Richard Hunt. Still in their early twenties, they have achieved reputations which evidently depend on more than the technological mood of the moment

Negro potters have produced much that is conventionally excellent. In their company Earl Hooks stands apart, for his transformations of biological shapes are attractively unique and colourful.

Barbara Chase
Victorious Bullfighter
BRONZE   1958

Plate 65
Courtesy Dr Perry Ottenburg,
Philadelphia

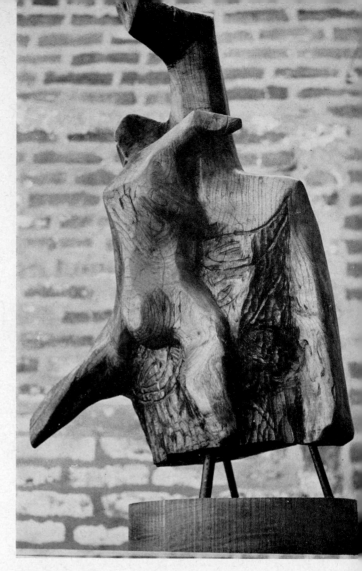

Adam and Eve
BRONZE 1958

Mother and Child
ORANGEWOOD 1956

Barbara Chase

The Last Supper
BRONZE 1958
Courtesy Ben Shahn

Plate 66

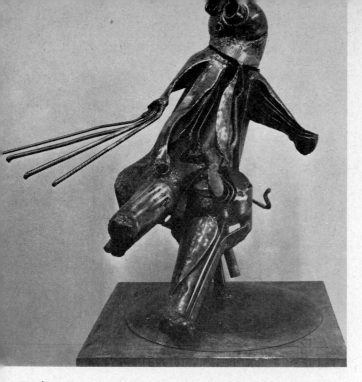

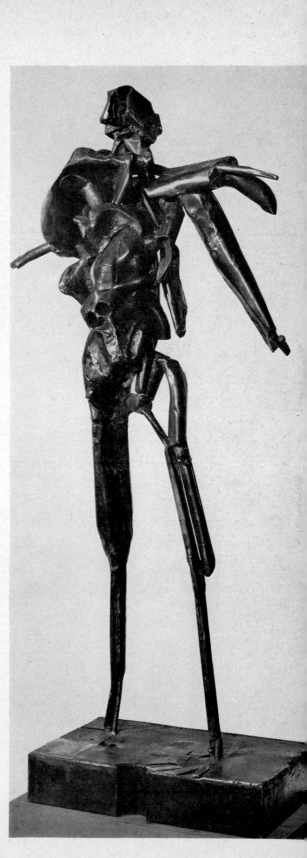

Arachne
STEEL   1956
*Courtesy Museum of
Modern Art, New York*

Plate 67

Richard Hunt

Hero Construction
STEEL   1958
*Courtesy the Art
Institute of Chicago*

Man on a Vehicle
SOLDERED METAL   1959
Courtesy Alan Gallery, New York

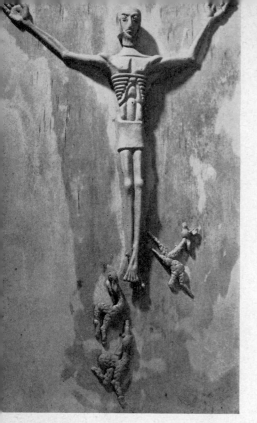

Carroll Simms
Christus and the Lambs
HAMMERED BRONZE   1956
In Tile Hill Church, Coventry

Angels
PLEXIGLASS   1952
*Courtesy Mrs Kenneth
Dale Owen, Houston*

Plate 68

Jack Jordan
Madonna and Child
1950
Courtesy Atlanta University

*The Musician
Courtesy Art Department
State University of Iowa*

Plate 69
Richmond Barthé
General Dessalines
Courtesy of the Artist
Photograph taken before
the statue was shipped to
Port-au-Prince, Haiti

Booker T. Washington 1945
In the Hall of Fame,
New York University

Wetta   1933
Courtesy Harmon Foundation

Shoe Shine Boy   1938
Courtesy Museum of Art, Oberlin
College, Ohio, and the Artist

Blackberry Woman   1932
Courtesy Whitney Museum of
American Art, New York

Feral Benga   1935

Mary
Courtesy I.B.M.

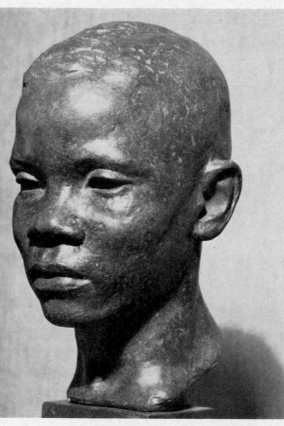

Plate 70

Richmond Barthé

Richmond Barthé
Ram Gopal (Dance of Siva)
Courtesy Alain Locke

Plate 71

Richmond Barthé
Laurence Olivier (Hotspur)
Courtesy the Artist

Augusta Savage
Lift Every Voice and Sing
The World Fair, 1939

Plate 72

Photo: *Carl Van Vechten*

Gregory Ridley
HEADS 1958
Courtesy Atlanta University

James Lewis
Frederick Douglass
Courtesy Morgan State
College, Baltimore, Md

Sargent Johnson
Forever Free
LACQUERED WOOD   1936

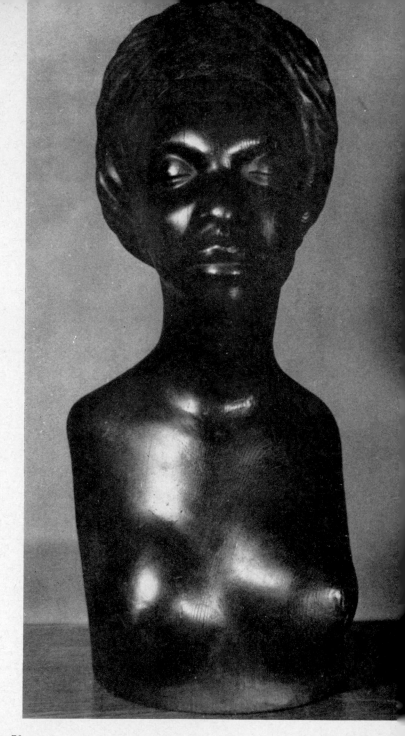

Plate 74

Sargent Johnson

Boy's Head
Girl's Head

TERRACOTTAS
Courtesy San Francisco
Museum of Art

Copper Mask 1929
Courtesy Dept. of Arts and Sciences,
International Business Machines Corp.

Guy Miller
Congo Beauty
WOOD   1952
Courtesy Atlanta
University

Plate 75

Elizabeth Catlett
Mother and Child

Photo: *M. Yampolsky*
Courtesy the Artist

Plate 76
William Artis
Heads
Courtesy Harmon Foundation

Courtesy Atlanta Univ.

Elizabeth Catlett
Negro Woman

Selma Burke
Temptation

Courtesy I.B.M.

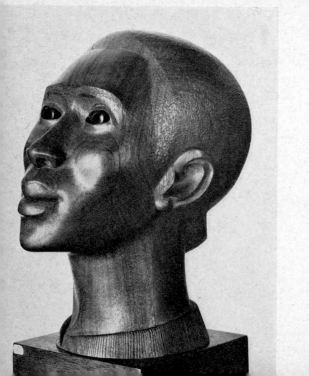

Plate 77

Ed Wilson
Minority Man
RED HICKORY   1957
Courtesy the Artist

Ed Wilson
Cybele
MARBLE
Trio
SYNTHETIC ALUMINIUM

Plate 78

Hayward Oubré
Mother and Child
Photo: *Elisha James*
Courtesy the Artist

Charles Alston
Torso
Courtesy I.B.M.

Joseph Kersey

St Francis
Courtesy Barnett
Aden Gallery

Young Girl
Courtesy James Porter

Marion Perkins
Don Quixote
Courtesy the Artist

Henry Bannarn
Portrait   1933 Harmon
John Brown   1941 I.B.M.
Daywork   1955 Atlanta

Man of Sorrow
Courtesy Art Institute of Chicago

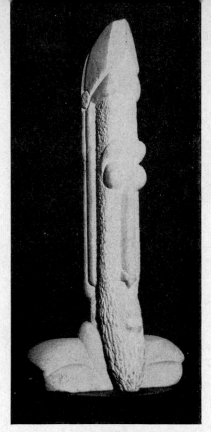

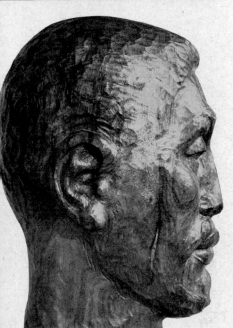

John Rhoden
Invictus
Courtesy United
Asia (Bombay)

Plate 79

Female Figure
Courtesy Atlanta
University

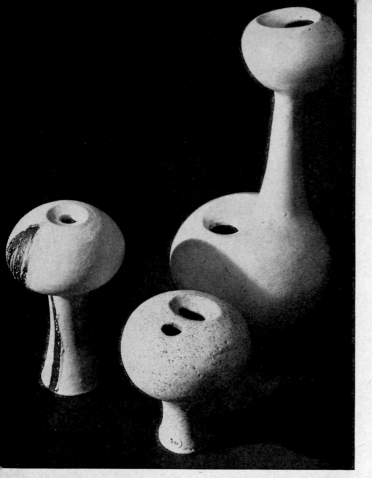

Plate 80

Earl Hooks

Vases
Bowls

Photos: *Lotte Lasker*
Courtesy the Artist

Jars and Dish
Vases

William Artis
Bowl
Courtesy Walker Art
Centre, Minneapolis

Alvin Hollingsworth
Waiting
Photograph: *Mike Herniter*
Courtesy the Artist

THE MODERN MANNER

Matisse declared that 'The painter must always feel that he is copying nature—and even when he consciously departs from nature, he must do it with the conviction that it is only the better to interpret her.' Most Negro artists share this opinion, with the added belief that social awareness and group-consciousness can be combined, when they urge expression, with creative vision and a personal manner.

But quite a few would probably agree with André Malraux that the truly modern painter rejects '*all* values that are not purely those of painting'. For them the purpose of painting is painting, though there might be added to it, sometimes, the hope of a pleasant ride on a popular bandwagon. It is a good way of making the worst of both possible worlds; for they cannot claim inclusion in any consideration of Negro art and there is a tendency to ignore them outside the Village—no Negro was included among the 113 artists whose works were shown in the exhibition of 'Modern Art in the United States' at the Tate Gallery in 1956.

Nevertheless, artists must paint as they wish and all good painting is important. The selection offered in the following plates has accordingly been guided only by the intention to illustrate the variety of the modern manner in American Negro art. That it leaves a slight feeling of interesting derivativeness was not calculated, nor has there been a prejudice against those who have entered 'the main stream of American art'. The fact is that most Negro artists are still at their best in interpretations and impressions, but there might have been more pictures that can be called 'non-representational' if the available photographs had met the need to do approximate justice to designed harmonies of colour.

Plate 81
Romare Bearden
He is Arisen
WATERCOLOUR AND INDIA INK   1945
Courtesy Museum of Modern Art, New York

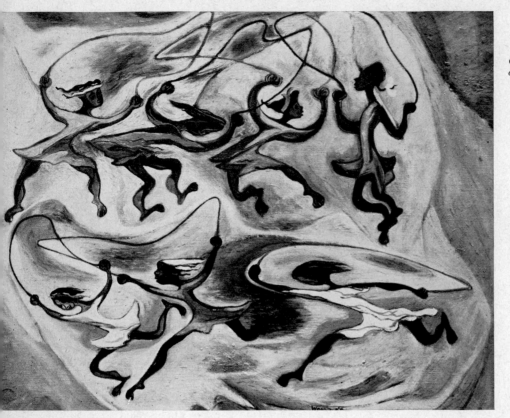

Plate 83 ▶

Jacob Lawrence

Tombstones
Courtesy Whitney Museum
of American Art, New York

Hale Woodruff

Girls Skipping
OIL   1949
Courtesy International
Business Machines Corp.

Plate 82

American Land
of Many Moons
OIL   1954
Courtesy the Artist

Alma Thomas
Still Life 1955
Courtesy Barnett Aden Gallery

Delilah Pierce
Daffodils
OIL 1958
*Courtesy Mr and Mrs John R.
Hoskins Jr. and the Artist*

Humbert Howard
The Yellow Cup
OIL 1950
*Courtesy The Pennsylvania
Academy of the Fine Arts*

Plate 84

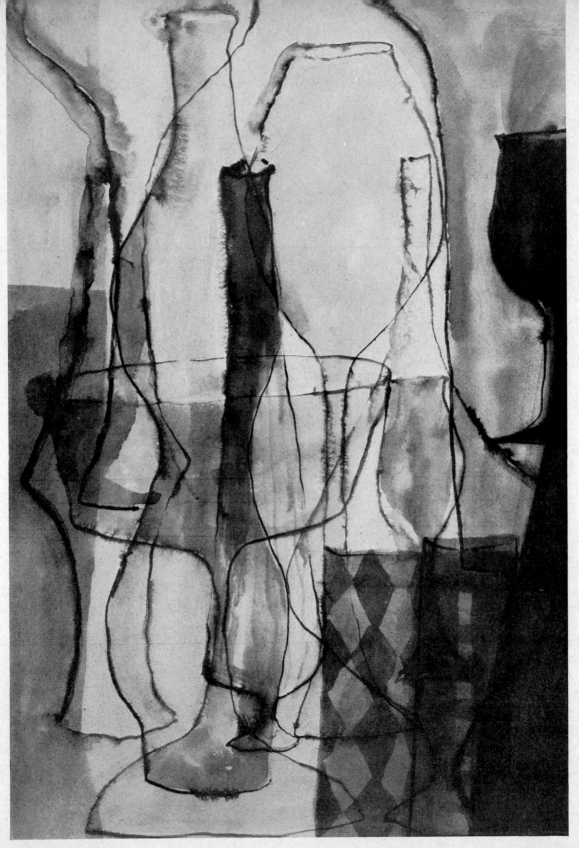

Stan Williamson
Glass Objects
INKS   1959

Walter Williams
Fighting Cock
COLOUR WOODCUT 1959
Courtesy The Studio

Poultry Market
OIL 1953
Courtesy Whitney Museum of
American Art, New York

Norma Morgan
Character Study 1957
Courtesy American Federation
of Arts through the Artist

Plate 90

Gilbert Harris
Nude
Courtesy the Artist

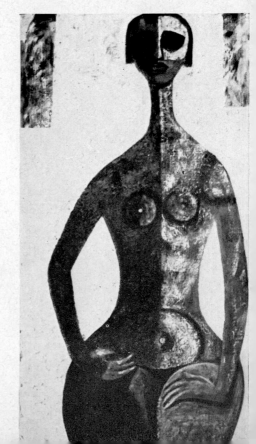

Plate 91

Charles Sebree
Ritual Woman
Art Institute of Chicago

Thomas Sills
Composition 1959
Courtesy the Artist

Barbara Chase
Bulls 1958
Galleria L'Oblisco, Rome

Harold Pierce
Debbie
Courtesy the Artist

Norman Lewis
Migrating Birds 1953
Courtesy Carnegie Institute
Pittsburg, Pa

Harper Phillips
Fisherman 1957
Courtesy Joseph Gilliard,
Hampton, Va

Alvin Hollingsworth
Flower Girl
Courtesy the Artist

Beauford DeLaney
Greene Street
OIL 1951
Courtesy Norman
Shoenfeld

Plate 92

Jacob Lawrence
The Negroes, who
had been part of the
soil for many years,
arrived in great
numbers in the urban
centres of the North.
From The Migration
of the Negro 1941
Courtesy The
Phillips Gallery,
Washington, D.C.

Plate 93
Walter Sanford
Susan and Friend
Courtesy the Artist

Eugene Grigsby
The Hunter
OIL   1959
Photo: *Stuart Weiner*
Courtesy Mrs Mimi Muth

Plate 94

Walter Sanford

Seated Nude 1959
Sun Ritual 1958
Courtesy the Artist

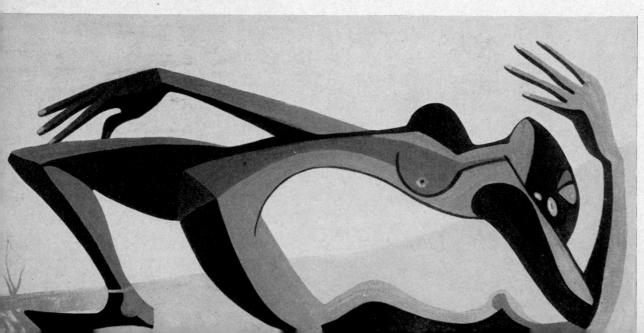

Plate 95
Rex Goreleigh
Jungle Dancer
WATERCOLOUR   1957
Courtesy the Artist

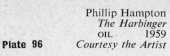

Phillip Hampton
The Harbinger
OIL   1959
Courtesy the Artist

Plate 96

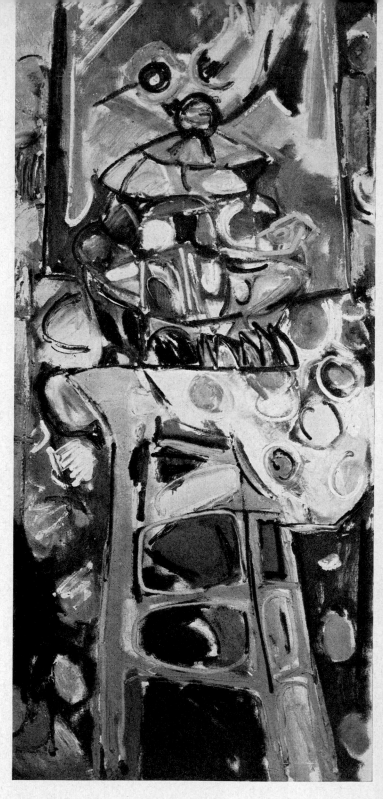

Mildred Thompson
The Emperor`s Nightingale
OIL   1958
Courtesy the Artist

Henry Tanner Barthe 1928
(Lake County Children's Home, Gary, Ind.)

Archibald Motley
David Jackson

Augusta Savage
Carl Van Vechten

Richmond Barthé
Harmon Foundation

Allan Freelon
Gaston Devigne

Plate 97

SOME OF
THE ARTISTS

Leslie Bolling
Kenneth Space

Sargent Johnson

◄ *Hale Woodruff*

William Johnson
Carl Van Vechten

James Wells

Rex Goreleigh
H. Halit

◄ *James Porter*

Alonzo Aden
Robert Scurlock

Romare Bearden

Ellis Wilson
Carl Van Vechten

Beauford DeLaney
Carl Van Vechten

Horace Pippin
Carl Van Vechten

Lois Mailou Jones
'Kay-Dee'

Delilah Pierce

Joseph Kersey

Jacob Lawrence
Carl Van Vechten

Richard Dempsey
Miller

Plate 98

Hughie Lee-Smith

Alma Thomas

Allan Crite

Henry Bannarn

William Walker

Yvonne Hunt
Charles Lowe

Frank Alston

Walter Simon
Arnowitz

John Howard

James Parks
Hammond Studio

Eldzier Cortor
Carl Van Vechten

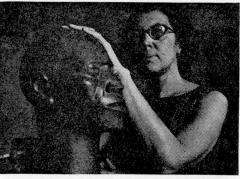

Elizabeth Catlett
M. Yampolsky

Harold Pierce

Earl Hooks (left)

Gilbert Harris

Robert Scurlock

Charles White
Robert Scurlock

William Artis
Wittekind

Plate 99

Alvin Hollingsworth

Eugenia Dunn

John Robinson

Ladybird Cleveland
Carl Van Vechten

James Washington

John Rhoden
USIS

Leedell Moorehead

Barbara Chase

Irene Clark
Jerry Coghill

Phillip Hampton

Marion Perkins

Roosevelt Woods

Norma Morgan
Trudie Fleischmann

Jewel Simon

Merton Simpson
Mel Mills

Jack Jordan

James Watkins

Claude Clark

Ed Wilson

Charles Stallings

June Hector

Gregory Ridley

John Wilson

Plate 100

Walter Sanford

Humbert Howard

ARTISTS AND PICTURES

182

183

184

GENERAL INDEX